PRINCIPLES OF BUSINESS FOR CXC

André L. Bernard

Other books from Cassell:

MCQ Office Procedures 0-304-31358-0

Office Procedures for the Caribbean, new edition 0-304-70508-X

Principles of Accounting for CXC 0-304-31038-7

Principles of Front Office Operations 0-304-32731-X

Principles of Business for CXC

FOURTH EDITION

DR SAM SEUNARINE
DBA, FCI, AFCS, AAPS, AMBIM, ACEA, ACFA, LLB, JD

Formerly Head of Business Studies Department,
St Benedict's College, La Romaine, Trinidad

CASSELL

Cassell

Wellington House
125 Strand
London WC2R 0BB

370 Lexington Avenue
New York
NY 10017-6550

First published 1980
Second edition 1986
Reprinted 1987, 1989
Third edition 1990
Reprinted eight times 1991–97
Fourth edition 1999

ISBN 0-304-70509-8

British Library Cataloguing in Publication Data
Seunarine, Sam
Principles of business for CXC – 4th ed.
1. Business
I. Title
II. Seunarine, Sam.
Principles of business for Caribbean Examinations Council examinations
650

Photographs by Liz Dash
Typeset by Kenneth Burnley, Wirral, Cheshire
Printed and bound in Great Britain by Biddles Ltd, Guildford and King's Lynn

Contents

Preface

This book has been written for use in all secondary and commercial schools in the Caribbean. It is designed for students preparing for the Caribbean Examinations Council (CXC) examinations in business studies. Those who are not preparing for any examination but who want to know something about the world of business today should also find the book useful and instructive.

From my 25 years' experience as a teacher in secondary schools and from a survey undertaken, I have found that students prefer to study short sections rather than long ones; and so this book consists of a number of short sections with, wherever possible, essential matter listed as numbered points.

The layout of the book follows the CXC syllabus closely. It should allow teacher and student to proceed with study of the contents in a logical order and it is suggested that the book be read through first. A detailed study should then be made, section by section. Each chapter is followed by numerous self-revision questions which should be attempted before moving on to the next chapter. As CXC Basic and General Proficiency examinations cater for a wide ability range, the questions have been made as varied as possible. Some are simple tests of factual recall; others are more searching and require calculation, discussion or research. An appendix of 99 multiple-choice questions should not only assist in testing a wide part of the syllabus, but also give valuable practice in answering this type of question, which forms an important part of the CXC examination.

My thanks go out to my wife, my mother and my children for their moral support. Without the help of these people, the book would not have been published.

This book has also been written with the invaluable help and suggestions of Mr Peter Turner.

DR SAM SEUNARINE

Couva, Trinidad, WI

April 1979, April 1986, March 1989 and February 1999

1

The nature of business and the business environment

The division of labour

In primitive societies, people did nearly everything themselves. They grew their own crops, made their own clothes and cooking pots, built their own houses. This was not very efficient; a good farmer may be a bad weaver, and some jobs never got done at all because people were so busy doing something else.

Gradually, each member of a community began to concentrate on doing one or two jobs only. One would be a farmer and trade surplus crops with a neighbour who was specializing in making tools, and so on. This is called *division of labour.*

The division of labour is a system whereby each person does the job for which he or she is best suited. In the eighteenth century, division of labour was taken a stage further, when the first large factories were set up. One job was split up into a number of processes with a different person in charge of each, all processes operating at the same time.

Adam Smith, the famous Scottish economist, gave a good example of this in his book *The Wealth of Nations.* He described how, in a pin factory, before there was division of labour, one man could produce only 20 pins a day, performing all the 18 processes necessary by himself. When the processes were split up among the 10 workers in the factory, 48,000 pins were produced per day. The output per worker was now 4,800 pins a day compared with 20 previously.

The *advantages* of division of labour are:

1. It leads to specialization and increase of skill. Doing the same job over and over makes people better at it.
2. Production is speeded up.
3. More use can be made of machines.
4. There is an increase in output.
5. There is usually an increase in quality.
6. Usually the cost per unit is less.

7. There will often be less use of manual labour. At the end of the day's work, the worker will be less tired.
8. Less time is needed in training the worker; this is to the benefit of both employer and employee.
9. Because of the savings in time and cost, the working week can be made shorter, and everyone enjoys a higher standard of living.
10. Management too can become more specialized. This is becoming a very important aspect of production.

The *disadvantages* are:

1. Work can become monotonous and boring.
2. Workers can lose pride in their work. No longer can a worker say 'That is *my* chair, I made it all myself.'
3. It can lead to bad relations between the employer and the employee. This is a serious problem in large factories like car assembly plants, where the workers have little control over their pace or style of work.

Despite its advantages, there are *limits to the possible division of labour:*

1. *The extent of the market.* If demand for a product is small, there will only be a living for a few people making it, so each person will have to do more than one job.
2. Some goods and services, by *the nature of the product,* mostly those involving specialist skill, have to be made, or at least co-ordinated, by one person, like drawing up a plan for a new building.
3. *Transport problems.* In remote areas, or small islands, people have to be 'jacks of all trades' if they want to get a job done quickly or cheaply. They cannot afford the time or money to call in a specialist from far away.
4. *Import restrictions.* Often a government will restrict specialization and division of labour by not allowing in products or workers from overseas, so as to give more work to its own people.
5. *Capital equipment.* Division of labour will often be restricted if a firm cannot afford to install special machinery.

Traditions have grown up whereby certain towns, districts or countries have specialized in the production of certain products. In Trinidad, Icacos and Mayaro are well known for their coconuts, and Caroni for sugar cane. On an international scale, Barbados is famous for its sugar cane, Jamaica for its coffee, Dominica for limes, Grenada for spices, Cuba for its cigars, and so on.

Business and commerce

We saw above that people soon began to exchange goods, services, or even just their labour, for other goods and services which they could not produce themselves, or which someone else could produce more cheaply. This is trade. Originally trade was restricted to dealing with friends and neighbours in the same town or village, or with passing strangers, but it has gradually grown in scope and complexity until today trade is world-wide. *Commerce* involves all those activities, procedures and institutions which make this trade possible (see Figure 1.1, page 6).

A *business* (or business unit) consists of a person or group of persons engaged in trade or some other commercial activity, with a view to making a profit by selling, trading, producing goods or services. Businesses can vary greatly in size. A small market trader is running a business; so are multi-million-dollar concerns such as General Motors. Businesses provide all the commercial services such as banking, insurance, warehousing, communications, advertising and transport, as well as the direct buying and selling, and import and export of goods. These will all be described in later chapters.

The words 'with a view to making a profit' are important. A church bazaar may be engaged in selling goods, but it is not a business, because the money made will be given to the church or charity. Nor is an amateur cricket team, a social club or a government department a business. Similarly, a private school, run for profit by its owners, is a business, but a state school, provided as a service to the community, is not. The various ways in which businesses are organized are described in Chapter 2.

Free enterprise, planned and mixed economies

Every country needs laws and regulations and must establish taxes to pay for services such as the armed forces, police, education and health services. The way this is done, and the effect that this has on the nation's business operations and material wealth (i.e. on its *economy*) differs from one country to another. There are three main types of economy in the modern world.

1. *A free enterprise economy*, as its name suggests, allows businesspeople the greatest possible freedom to run their business in the way they think best. Nearly all resources are privately owned, and the consumer, who can afford it, has unrestricted freedom of choice. The market is free and very competitive, and there are very few government controls. Largely because it does not provide any protection for the poor, the old and the ill, a system like this is very rare today.

The nearest to a free enterprise economy is probably the United States of America.

2. *A planned economy* has all its production and distribution planned and controlled by the state, which also owns all the factories and shops. It is usually associated with socialism or communism. A good example of a planned economy is Cuba.
3. *A mixed economy* is so called because it has a mixture of state and private ownership. A limited free market exists side by side with a lot of government planning and regulation. Such a system exists in most of the islands of the Caribbean.

The public and private sectors of the economy

The *public sector* refers to the government-owned industries (such as public transport, electricity, etc.) and services affecting business (such as harbours, post office services, etc.)

The *private sector* refers to privately-owned businesses within the country.

Both the public and the private sectors require finance. The private sector will raise the funds needed to start its business and buy capital equipment and premises, by raising private or bank loans or by selling shares. The public sector will sell government bonds and Treasury Bills to raise capital. Shares issued by the private sector in the Caribbean are usually taken up very quickly, on the day of issue; many are oversubscribed. Many people, on the other hand, are hesitant about investing in government bonds and Treasury Bills, even though some of them are issued with interest paid tax-free.

The public sector of the economy can influence the private sector in three ways:

1. By competing for available investment funds, as described above. If the government wants a lot of money, this tends to drive interest rates up, as the investor can pick and choose where to put his money. If a business has to pay high interest rates, its costs are increased, and it is more difficult for it to make a profit. This may discourage people from expanding their businesses.
2. By the government's general management of the economy. Obviously, it is easier for the private sector if the economy is stable and prosperous. If, on the other hand, there is no confidence in future prosperity, or if there is a lot of unemployment or inflation, business will be depressed.
3. By the efficiency with which public services such as postal deliveries, telephones, docks and customs are run. They may be run by

people appointed by the government for various political reasons, or civil servants with no business training or experience. Many such services are notoriously inefficient, in the Caribbean and elsewhere, and if private industries (which have to pay their way and make a profit) were run on such lines, they would soon go bankrupt. This is not so with public services, where losses are paid for by higher taxation or higher charges.

However, the public sector provides many vital services which have to be continued whether they make a profit or not, such as water supply, hospitals, refuse collection, sewage treatment, etc. The main aim of the public sector is not to make a profit but to serve the country.

Both the public and private sectors are important in the economic growth of the Caribbean territories. Without public services, the private sector could not conduct its business. Without the wealth created by the private sector, the government could not raise the money needed to run the public services.

Types of productive activity

There are three main types of productive activity – *industry, direct services* and *commerce*. Commerce has already been mentioned.

Direct services are provided by those who do not produce goods, but perform a service which is useful to their fellows. Examples are teachers, lawyers, doctors, nurses and soldiers. Although they do not produce goods themselves, their work is productive because without their services other people, who do produce goods, would not be able to do their work.

Industries can be divided into four main types:

1. *Extractive industries.* All industries which are engaged in obtaining raw materials are extractive industries. Examples are quarrying, fishing, mining and farming. These were the earliest forms of industry and are still the foundation-stone on which all other occupations are built.
2. *Manufacturing industries.* These include all those engaged in changing the form of the things produced by extractive industries and making them useful to man. For example, in a brickworks, clay (which is not much use by itself) is shaped and baked into bricks. In an ironworks iron ore is smelted and made into iron or steel, which may then be further processed to make it into galvanized sheeting or tin cans.
3. *Construction and building industries.* These take the various components made by manufacturing industry and perhaps some of the

products of extractive industry (like sand or stone) and build them up into an organized whole, like a house. The various parts of a motor car are manufactured from raw materials at a number of different factories (they are then called *components*). The tyres, batteries, upholstery, nuts, bolts, radiators, mufflers and so on are then transported to an assembly plant and made into motor cars.

4. *Service industries*, which include such things as transport, garages, repair shops, communications and tourism.

The various productive activities are illustrated in the diagram (Figure 1.1).

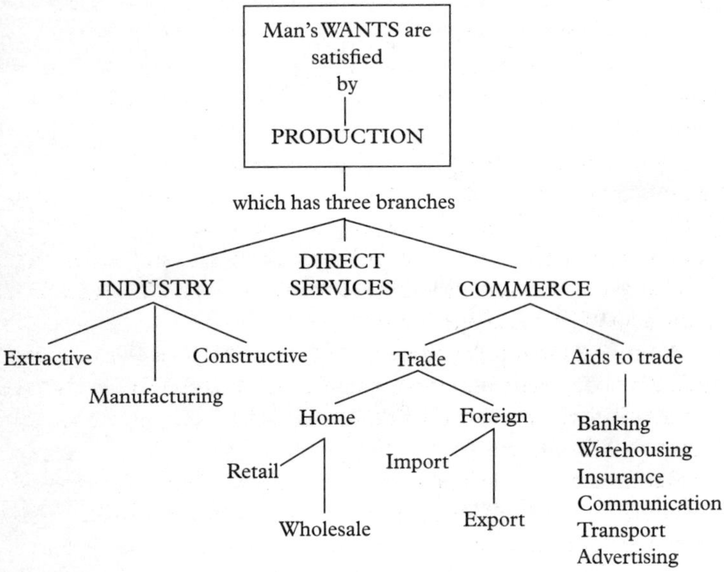

Figure 1.1 Branches of production

Industries of the Caribbean

In the past, nearly all industry in the Caribbean was extractive – farming, fishing, forestry and mining for oil and minerals. The raw materials were consumed locally or exported in exchange for imported manufactured goods. Extractive industries are still very important, but more and more manufacturing industries have been set up. There are also construction industries such as car assembly plants, although many of the components still have to be imported from outside the Caribbean.

It is difficult to say where exactly these industries are located, since most of them are to be found all over the islands, which all have a very similar climate and can grow the same crops if they want to. If we take Trinidad as an example, we find that there are over 600 different industries, some large, some small. Some are linked with other industries. Much the same is true of Jamaica. It is in mining that the main differences are found between the Caribbean countries. Trinidad has a large and important oil industry. No oil has yet been found in Jamaica, but it has important deposits of bauxite (the raw material from which aluminium is made).

Sugar cane is the most important agricultural crop of the Caribbean. Unfortunately it faces strong competition from the beet sugar grown in Western Europe and the USA. Demand for it and its by-product, rum, has fallen off and in many cases the price obtained for it scarcely covers the cost of production; but governments still encourage sugar-cane growing, either because their countries have little else to sell in world markets, or because it employs so many workers who would otherwise be out of a job.

Other crops grown are bananas, coconuts (grown for copra as well as for oil), cocoa, coffee, limes and other citrus fruits, pineapples and spices – all of which are exported – as well as maize and vegetables grown for local consumption. There are also food processing industries: sugar is not exported in its raw state, but is made into refined sugar, molasses or rum; a lot of fruit is canned; and so on.

An important industry throughout the Caribbean is tourism, which is well developed, with hundreds of first-class hotels and other facilities to attract visitors. This is a service industry which brings in a considerable amount of foreign currency.

Recently some Caribbean governments have begun to control the location of industry. There are two main reasons for this. The first is to stop pollution and spoilage of attractive scenery. The second is to encourage industrial development away from traditional centres, so as to spread employment opportunities more evenly and reduce congestion. For example, in Trinidad the docks at Port of Spain and the roads all round the capital have become badly overloaded; by building new docks further down the coast, the government hopes to attract more industry to the less congested south of the island.

Scale

Compared with those in Europe, the USA, or Japan, most industries in the Caribbean are on a small scale. Even Trinidad's oil industry is small when compared with those of Venezuela or Saudi Arabia. This is because the population of most Caribbean islands is small and they cannot provide a sufficient market for large, complicated or specialized industries which depend for efficiency on economies of scale (see Chapter 6). In other cases, as with paper production, the raw materials needed are not available and it is cheaper to import the finished product than bulky raw materials. Thus although industrialization is well advanced in the larger islands, and will continue to expand, there will always be a need for imported manufactured goods, which will have to be largely paid for by export of raw materials (oil, minerals, etc.) or agricultural products.

RESEARCH ACTIVITY

Draw a map of your country and mark where the major industries are.

SELF-REVISION QUESTIONS

1. Explain what is meant by the division of labour. What are its advantages and disadvantages?
2. What are the limits to the division of labour? Illustrate your answer, if possible, with examples from your own territory of where specialization is not likely to take place.
3. What are the advantages of large-scale production? Why is it not tried out more widely in the Caribbean?
4. Define a business. Name *six* organizations in your territory which are businesses, and six that are not.
5. What is the difference between industry and commerce?
6. What are the main classifications of industry? Do you think that one is more important to the local economy than the others?
7. Name some of the important industries of your territory and say where they are to be found.
8. Explain the difference between a mixed and a controlled economy. Are there any controlled economies in the Caribbean?
9. How does a country obtain and pay for the goods which it can produce locally?

2

The internal organizational structure of business

There are seven main types of business structure. The essential difference between them is the *form of ownership.* These seven types are:

- the sole trader;
- the partnership;
- the co-operative;
- limited companies (including conglomerates, holding companies and multi-nationals);
- state corporations and nationalized industries;
- government departments;
- local and municipal authorities.

The essential differences between them are summed up in Table 2.1.

Type of business	*Owned by*	*Run by*	*Liability**
Sole trader	One proprietor	The owner himself *or* a manager appointed by *him*	Unlimited
Partnership	Two or more partners	The partners (some or all)	Unlimited
Limited company	No one. The company is a 'legal person' which owns its own assets.	Board of directors appointed by the shareholders	Limited
Co-operative	The members	Management committee elected by the members	Unlimited
State corporations and nationalized industries	The nation	Board of directors appointed by the government	Unlimited
Government departments	Central government	Public servants, permanent secretary	People
Local and municipal authorities	Regional, borough, city council	Minister of government	People

*For an explanation of liability, see the section on companies below.

Table 2.1 The seven main types of business structure

The sole trader

A sole trader's business is owned entirely by one man or woman alone ('sole' means 'alone'). It does not necessarily mean that he runs his business single-handed – he may employ staff or have his family to help him – but he has provided all the capital, he must be responsible for all the important decisions, and if his business does badly and he cannot pay his debts from the business assets, then he may have to sell off his house or private possessions to raise the cash.

The sole trader is a very common type of business. It is the easiest of all to start up. Any adult can do this (provided he can raise the capital) and there are no legal formalities, although a licence may be required to operate certain types of business.

Most businesses of this type are small, since the capital of one man is limited. The most common types of sole trader are shopkeepers and self-employed craftsmen, repair-men, taxi drivers, etc.

Most of the advantages and disadvantages of the sole trader are the same as those of any small business, which are described in Chapter 6. But there are three further disadvantages to be mentioned. The first is unlimited liability for the business's debts. The second is that if the owner dies or falls ill, the business usually collapses – it can be difficult to find a buyer. The third is that the owner may have to pay a lot of income tax, and may find it difficult to plough back enough profits into the business. For these reasons, there is a tendency for some more prosperous sole traders to turn their businesses into limited companies.

Partnership

A partnership is like a sole trader's business, except that there are several owners (partners) carrying on the business together, sharing the risks and the profits. Again they may employ other staff, who are not partners. Once again there are very few formalities, except that the name of the business must be registered unless it consists simply of the names of all the partners. All the partners are fully responsible for the business's debts, and if one partner cannot pay his share, then the loss will fall on the other partner or partners.

The partners can make whatever arrangements they like between themselves on the running of the business and sharing the profits. It is always wise to have a written partnership agreement or *deed.* This saves a lot of argument if disputes arise between the partners later. No partnership deed exists, or if it does not cover the particular point at issue, and the matter comes before the courts, then the law assumes that the rules laid down in the British Partnership Act of 1890 apply. These are:

1. Profits and losses will be shared equally among all the partners.
2. All partners can bind the business, e.g. place orders for goods which will then have to be paid for out of partnership funds.
3. No interest will be paid on partners' capitals, or charged on drawings (money they have withdrawn from the business).
4. No partner will be entitled to any salary.

In practice, these rules are often altered in the partnership deed. Some partners may contribute a larger capital than others; it is quite common to allocate profits in proportion to capital, or to allow interest on capital. Some partners (known as sleeping partners) may only contribute capital but take no active part in the running of the business to compensate the partners that do, the latter may be paid a salary in addition to their share of profits.

The advantages of a partnership over a sole proprietorship are that larger capital can be employed and the work of management shared out – some of the partners may be experts or possess between them knowledge which no one person could have. The disadvantages are much the same as a sole trader's – unlimited liability for the firm's debts, possible difficulty when a partner dies or retires, and unfavourable tax treatment. (There is a special kind of partnership, the limited partnership, where some, but not all, partners may put a limit on their liability, but this has never been popular.) For these reasons, progressive businesspeople tend to favour the limited company rather than the partnership. Most partnerships today are found among architects, lawyers, accountants and other professionals whose code of conduct does not permit them to limit their liability.

The limited company

The limited company is so called because the liability of the owners (the shareholders) for the company's debts is *limited* to the amount of capital that they have subscribed (or agreed to subscribe, if the shares they have taken out have not been fully paid for). Invention of the limited company in the nineteenth century was a great step forward, because it enabled a much wider range of people to invest in business without having to take any part in its day-to-day management, yet knowing exactly the maximum amount that they stood to lose should the business fail. At the same time, because of the company's limited liability, the public at large, particularly those who have lent the company money or supplied it with goods or services on credit, need extra protection against loss and so the rules governing limited companies are much stricter than for partnerships or sole traders.

In fact there are other types of company besides the limited company. These are shown in Figure 2.1 – but the private and public limited companies are the only ones with which we shall be concerned in this book.

Starting a company

Before a new company can be incorporated, a number of documents must be drawn up and deposited with the Registrar of Companies (senior government official).

1. *Memorandum of association.* This states:
   (a) The name of the company (with 'Limited' as the last word). The Registrar may refuse to accept the name if he thinks it misleading, or if it is the same as, or could be confused with, the name of another company already on the Register.

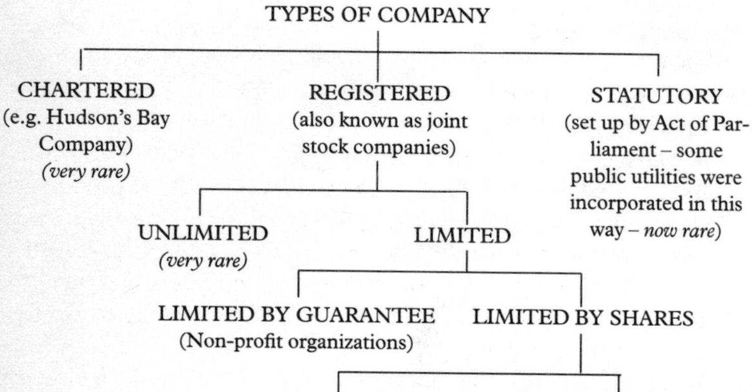

	PUBLIC LIMITED COMPANIES	PRIVATE LIMITED COMPANIES
No. of shareholders	Minimum 7, no maximum	Minimum 2, maximum 50*
Shares	May be offered for sale to the public May be traded on a stock exchange (if company has a 'quotation' on the stock exchange)	May not be offered for sale to the public Cannot be traded on a stock exchange

* with certain exceptions

Figure 2.1 Types of company

(b) Where the registered office of the company will be situated.
(c) The objects of the company, i.e. what it is being formed to do. A company's actions will not be recognized by the law (declared *ultra vires* or 'beyond its powers') unless they fall within the terms of the objects clause. The objects clause, therefore, should not be made too restrictive.
(d) That the liability of the members is limited.
(e) The amount of capital with which the company proposes to be registered, and the type of shares with which it will be made up.

At the end comes the 'association clause', a declaration signed by at least two of the prospective shareholders (seven in the case of a public company), stating that they desire to be formed into a company and number of shares they will each take.

2. *Articles of association.* These consist of detailed regulations governing the conduct of the company's business and the internal management of the company. These must be signed by the subscribers to the memorandum of association, and witnessed. Many companies adopt the standard form of articles embodied in most countries' Companies Acts. The memorandum and articles are often combined into the same booklet.
3. *Statement of authorized or nominal capital.* This is usually included under 1(e) above.
4. *A prospectus.* This is only required by public companies, intending to offer their shares for sale to the public. This includes details of how the company will operate, and an application form. (This must be passed by a stock exchange if the shares are to be traded here.) If a private company wishes to turn itself into a public company (called 'going public'), the prospectus will contain details of the company's assets and trading history.
5. When the Registrar has approved the documents and the necessary fees have been paid, he issues a *certificate of incorporation.* Without this certificate, the company cannot enter into valid contracts.

A private company may now commence trading, but a public company will also require:

6. *A certificate of trading* (also called a certificate to commence business). This is issued by the Registrar when he receives a declaration from the directors that the formalities concerned with the issue of shares have been complied with. Before this is issued a public company may not trade but may only incur expenses such as printing, advertising or postage necessary for the issue of shares.

It has already been noted that a company obtains its capital by the issue of shares. These are of two main types:

1. *Ordinary shares.* The rate of dividend paid on these shares is not fixed, but is decided every year by the shareholders at an annual general meeting. As dividends can only be paid out of profits or reserves (accumulated profits from previous years), in a good year ordinary shareholders will do well, but when little or no profit is made, they may get no dividend at all (this is called 'passing' the dividend).
2. *Preference shares.* These carry a fixed rate of dividend, but again this can only be paid out of profits or reserves. They are so called because preference shareholders get their dividend *in preference* to ordinary shareholders when profits are low. *Cumulative preference shares* carry a right to make up arrears of interest passed in previous years, when profits are sufficient to make this possible, before anything is paid to ordinary shareholders.

Only ordinary shareholders are entitled to vote at general meetings of the company. Besides approving the final dividends on the ordinary shares, they must approve the audited accounts and elect (or re-elect) the directors. In practice, very few shareholders in large public companies exercise their right to attend general meetings. All companies have ordinary shares; only some have preference shares, and there may be different categories (1st preference, 2nd preference, etc.), carrying different rates of interest.

The Registrar will approve the issue of a certain number of shares of a certain *par or nominal value* (for example, 100,000 ordinary shares of $1 each, giving an authorized capital of $100,000). It is normal practice today to invite applications (or arrange the placing in the case of a private company) for an issue of shares, and to demand payment of the whole nominal value with applications; this reduces administrative costs and discourages speculators. But the capital can be issued, and payment for each share made, by instalments. Suppose in the example above the company decided to issue only half its authorized capital and to demand only 40¢ on each $1 share on application, then the position would be:

	$
Authorized capital (100,000 shares of $1)	100,000
Issued capital (50,000 shares of $1)	50,000
Paid-up capital (40¢ on 50,000 shares)	20,000

Should the company run into financial difficulties, each shareholder may be required to contribute up to 60¢ per share to help clear its debts, i.e. up to the limit of their liability, which is the nominal value of $1 per share. They may also be required to pay up the balance of 60¢ at any time if the company decides to make another *call.*

The price at which shares can be bought or sold (their *market value)* will often differ significantly from the par value, up or down, according to how well or badly the company is doing. Suppose now that the company in the example above decides to issue its remaining 50,000 shares because it wants more capital to expand its business. It is doing well and the market value of its shares is $1.25. It is clearly wrong to sell the new shares for only $1 each; instead they will probably be sold for $1.25, or at a *premium* of 25¢. The authorized and paid-up capital will then be the same, but can still only be $100,000. The extra $12,500 received from the premium of 25¢ per share will be placed in a special *share premium reserve.* The company could, instead, give existing shareholders first refusal of the new shares; it would then be called a *rights* issue, since each shareholder would have the right to buy one new share for each one already held.

If the company were doing badly, it might wish to issue the new shares at a *discount,* i.e. for less than the nominal value, since no one would want them at the full price. However, this would leave it with a nominal capital which would not be backed by actual cash receipts; this might be misleading to the public. So issuing shares at a discount is not allowed without the approval of the High Court.

A company may also raise working capital through loans. The interest on these loans must be paid and deducted before arriving at the net profit available for distribution to shareholders. The loan may be broken down into small units and offered for sale to the public as *debentures.* These may seem rather like preference shares, but the differences are:

Preference shares	*Debentures*
Part of the company's share capital.	A loan (long-term liability).
Receive a fixed rate of dividend, which can only be paid out of profits or reserves.	Receive a fixed rate of interest, which must be paid whether a profit is made or not.
Only repaid when the company is wound up.	May be repayable on a specific date.
(If the company becomes insolvent, and cannot pay its debts:) Shareholders receive nothing until all other creditors have been paid.	Debenture-holders (if secured) receive preference over trade creditors.

Debentures are sometimes issued in blocks as *loan stock.*

The company is run by a *board of directors* appointed by the shareholders. The director who presides at board meetings is called the *chairman* or *president.* Directors may be responsible for the day-to-day running of the business, when they are known as *executive* or *working directors* (the chief executive among them is known as the *managing director*); or they may not take any active part in running the business except at board meetings, when they are known as *outside* or *non-executive directors.* Each company must also have a *secretary,* who may or may not also be a director. He is responsible for seeing that annual general meetings are called according to law, that proper minutes of annual general and board meetings are kept, for maintaining the company's share register and for ensuring that the books of account prescribed by law are kept, audited and published.

For the protection of investors and suppliers, every company must publish accounts giving certain prescribed information. A copy of these accounts must be deposited with the government, which will allow them to be inspected by the public for a small fee. The company's share register may also be inspected by the public. It must state the owners and registered numbers of all the company's shares; no sale and transfer of shares is legally valid until it has been recorded in the register.

These legal requirements may seem complicated, but they soon become a matter of routine in well-managed companies. A solicitor will attend to the formalities of registration, if required, and advise a small company on its legal obligations. The main disadvantage of the limited company is some increase in paperwork and administrative costs. The advantages are:

1. It is much easier to raise capital, since a wider circle of investors will be willing to invest money because their liability in case of failure will be limited.
2. The capital of a limited company can be much greater, and its operations on a much larger scale, than those of a sole trader or partnership.
3. It is much easier to buy and sell shares, in large or small blocks, than a partner's or sole trader's holding.
4. A company is a separate legal entity from its shareholders, and is not directly affected by their death, retirement, illness or bankruptcy.
5. Large companies can offer different types of investment to the public.
6. Large companies can benefit from the advantages of scale (see Chapter 3).
7. Companies often have tax advantages.

Conglomerates

When two or more companies join or merge in the same country, they are referred to as a conglomerate. They may be producing similar, related or unrelated goods and/or services.

Holding companies

As the name suggests, this is a company that 'holds' – or 'owns' as it is popularly known in the Caribbean – the majority of shares in another company (called a subsidiary company). The parent company is called the holding company. The subsidiaries usually use their own names and carry on their own affairs, but general administrative control is held by the holding company.

Multi-national corporations

These are just like holding companies but they operate in many countries of the world. Sometimes the government of the country dictates the terms and conditions of their presence in that country and how they should operate.

Co-operatives

There are two main types of co-operative, producer co-operatives and consumer co-operatives. The former are voluntary groups of small farmers who co-operate to sell their produce to the factories and the markets at a better price.

Consumer co-operatives originated in 1844 in Rochdale, England. At that time working men and women were often cheated by dishonest traders who charged very high prices, put sand in the brown sugar and so on. Twenty-eight weavers in Rochdale got together and founded the Rochdale Co-operative Society. They set up shop and sold honest goods (mostly foodstuffs) to the working people of Rochdale at reasonable prices. The idea soon spread and co-operative societies sprang up all over England, Wales and Scotland. Later they set up the Co-operative Wholesale Society (CWS) to manufacture items such as polish and soap for sale in the co-operative shops. The co-operative movement also sponsors MPs who support the Labour Party in the British House of Commons. The four principles on which the co-operative movement is based are:

1. *Open membership.* All members of the public can join for a very small fee.

2. *Democratic control.* All major decisions are taken by meetings of members. The members also elect a committee to see to the day-to-day running of the society. Each member only has one vote, irrespective of the amount of capital he has subscribed. (This is not like a company, where a shareholder's voting rights depend on the number of ordinary shares he owns.)
3. *Limited interest* on capital invested – seldom more than 5%.
4. *Profit-sharing.* All profits not ploughed back into the business are distributed to members *in proportion to their purchases* during the year (again unlike a company, where profits are distributed in proportion to capital invested). This used to be done by recording purchases in a book and declaring a 'dividend' of so much per cent at the end of a year; now members are given trading stamps with their purchases which they can either convert into cash or use to buy more goods.

The co-operatives have now stopped expanding. They face strong competition from supermarkets and other large retail chains. Sometimes they are not as well run as private shops because they are unable to pay enough to attract top-class managers and because members of the management committee are not expert in business. However, some societies are fighting back by opening larger, more attractive stores and offering a wider range of merchandise. All types of goods are sold – furniture, clothes, electrical equipment, hardware – but about 80% of the trade is in foodstuffs. There is also a Co-operative Bank and a co-operative funeral service.

Nationalized industries

A nationalized industry is an organization (usually very large) engaged in commerce or industrial production and owned by the nation. It is run by the government, who appoint a chairman and board of directors to manage it. There is usually a government minister responsible to Parliament for each nationalized industry (some ministers may be responsible for several industries).

Many nationalized industries were formerly *public utility companies* providing utilities (essential services) such as gas, electricity or water. To do this job effectively, they had to be given special powers (for instance, to lay pipes under the roads or to run electric power lines over private property, whether the owner objected or not). They were also protected from competition – it would be absurd for two companies to supply electricity to the same street. In recent years, most countries have thought it best for such services to be under direct government control, so these industries were nationalized (taken over by the government). When this happens, the shareholders usually receive government stock in return for their shares; they receive interest on this stock irrespective of whether the industry makes a profit and they have no more say in how the industry is run.

Other industries may also be taken over because it is thought important to have them under direct government control. The following industries are often nationalized in the Caribbean (and elsewhere):

- Postal services.
- Telephone service.
- Railways and bus services.
- Air services.
- Electricity, gas and water supply.
- Ports, harbours, and airports.

However, some industries are nationalized in one Caribbean country and not in another: the telephone service is nationalized in Trinidad but not in Barbados, for instance. Countries such as Guyana with a more controlled economy will have more nationalized industries than other countries. The aims of nationalization are:

1. To transfer the profits of the industry from private shareholders to the community at large.
2. To revitalize a declining industry with fresh investment.
3. To protect a vital but loss-making industry from closure.
4. To start up a new industry when private enterprise is unable or unwilling to do so.
5. To concentrate all the major means of production, distribution and exchange in state hands.

Nationalization is always controversial and strongly linked with politics. It is usually favoured more by socialist than non-socialist parties. Those who are for it naturally emphasize its advantages, and those who are against, because they believe in free enterprise, will stress its drawbacks. Among the benefits of nationalization may be:

1. Safeguarding of industries and jobs in them.
2. Improved working conditions.
3. Increased investment. This can have a 'knock-on' effect in bringing more trade to suppliers of goods and services to the industry.
4. More regard for the social consequences of industrial processes – for instance, better compensation for those injured at work.

By grouping several small firms into one large unit, the industry may become more competitive in overseas markets.

Problems may arise, however. If the management of the industry is weak, a heavy burden may fall on the taxpayer, who will have to make good the industry's losses. The monopolistic nature of nationalized industries makes it very difficult to measure efficiency and may lead to a 'take it or leave it' attitude to the consumer. Quality and variety of output may suffer. Although in theory each nationalized industry is responsible to a government minister and through him to Parliament, there is some doubt in practice how far the minister and the MPs can exercise control over very specialized and complicated operations.

Government departments

When Parliament has passed the necessary legislation, the main instrument for giving effect to government policy is one or other government department. These usually work in collaboration with local authorities and the nationalized industries. A change of government will not have any effect on the general functioning or staffing of a government department, although there can be changes in the organization structure.

A minister (sometimes called a parliamentary secretary) is put at the head of each government department. He or she is a politician appointed by the Head of State on the advice of the Prime Minister as part of the government. Most (but not all) ministers are also members of the Cabinet. If the government is defeated or loses its majority at a general election, then the minister will be replaced by one from another party. He is responsible for seeing that government policy is carried out so far as his own ministry is concerned. He will probably not be an expert in the subject of his department.

The minister is assisted by a staff of permanent civil servants, who are government employees. The chief civil servant in each department is usually called the permanent secretary. The civil servants are responsible for carrying into effect the details of legislation, and for advising the minister on the likely effects of any proposed changes.

Most senior civil servants are 'generalists', that is to say they will be expected to serve in any government department to which they may be posted. Many departments also have professionally qualified specialists, such as legal and financial advisers. In the smaller islands of the Caribbean, however, it is usual to have one legal and financial department to advise all other departments. Many government departments are assisted by advisory bodies, made up of outside experts serving part-time in addition to their regular jobs; sometimes they are paid, sometimes the posts are honorary (unpaid). Examples would be committees examining the safety of drugs or advising on the weapons which should be bought for the armed forces. *Ad hoc* (temporary) committees are also set up from time to time to do a specific job, examine a problem which is causing concern, and make recommendations. Their recommendations may be accepted by the government, either in whole or in part; or the government may take no action.

The division into government departments or ministries will vary from one country to another, but the following usually exist in all countries:

1. The *Treasury* (or Ministry of Finance). Responsible for ensuring that enough money is raised through taxation and loans. It is usually also responsible for the allocation of funds to other departments and for the recruitment and training of civil servants.
2. The tax-collection departments, usually divided into two parts, the *Inland Revenue* (responsible for income, corporation and capital gains taxes), and *Customs and Excise* (responsible for import and excise duties and sales taxes).
3. The *Home Office* (or Ministry of Home Affairs). Responsible for public order, immigration, law courts, the police, fire services and prisons.
4. The *Foreign Ministry*, responsible for the country's relations with other countries and its embassies and high commissions abroad.
5. The *Ministry of Defence*, responsible for the army, navy and air force.
6. The *Ministry of Education.*
7. The *Ministry of Health*, responsible for hospitals, medical services and the training of doctors and nurses.
8. The *Ministry of Trade* (or *Commerce*). Responsible for the government's dealings with industry, the regulation of business and consumer protection.
9. The *Ministry of Agriculture.*

Local authorities

Under the authority of the Parliament of the country, local authorities may be set up to deal with matters of local concern. Their powers, duties and functions are defined by an Act of Parliament. They are elected by those who live in the area concerned. Each consists of a council with a chairman or mayor at its head, who presides over meetings of the council and represents the town or district on important occasions, such as the opening of a new hospital or sports stadium. Besides the elected councillors there may also be a small number of aldermen, usually senior councillors who are not directly elected but nominated by the other members of the council.

The powers of the local authorities (variously known as counties, parishes or boroughs) will vary from one country to another. They are usually responsible for such things as water supply, drainage, sewers, refuse disposal, street cleaning, community health services and sports facilities. Each main function is usually controlled by a committee of the main council, but its decisions have to be ratified (approved) by the main council. The council is served by a staff of permanent officials and council workers, who carry out the decisions of the council and advise the councillors on what they should do.

Local councils obtain their finance through central government grants and rates (property taxes). The central government ensures that the money is properly spent by employing auditors whose job it is to examine and check the local authorities' accounts. Local authorities play an important role in the commercial and economic development of the country.

Major functional areas in business

In all except the smallest business, where the proprietor will closely supervise (or actually carry out) all the different operations himself, division of labour takes place. For convenience the business is divided into specialized departments, each with its own experts. The chief of these are:

1. *Production.* This is concerned with manufacturing or processing the goods which the business sells. Naturally this department will not exist where the business is engaged only in retailing or wholesaling (buying and selling already manufactured goods), or in a service industry.
2. *Finance* (or accounts department). This keeps the firm's books of account, pays the wages and other bills, receives money from customers, and ensures that sufficient cash is always available for the day-to-day running of the business and financing capital expenditure.
3. *Marketing.* This is particularly important in large organizations, who have to ensure that they do not lose touch with the consumer. It is the function of the marketing department to *discover and satisfy the needs of the customers at a profit.* It therefore includes market research and product development as well as selling, advertising and distribution.
4. *Personnel.* This recruits, trains and looks after the welfare of staff and workers. It may also negotiate with trade unions.

The way in which firms organize and label these functions varies considerably. A large firm will have more departments than a medium-sized one. However, all four functions (except sometimes the first) have to be carried out, however organized. Different systems of organization will be considered in the rest of this chapter.

Organizational structure

Organizational structure may be defined as 'a formal, well-planned relationship between the personnel in an organization and the functions they perform in relation to other personnel and the objectives of the organization'. This may be put more simply as 'working out what everybody in an organization should do'. Organizational structure is often difficult to understand in the abstract and is therefore usually presented in the form of *organization charts*.

Organizational structures fall into three main groups: line, staff and functional organizations.

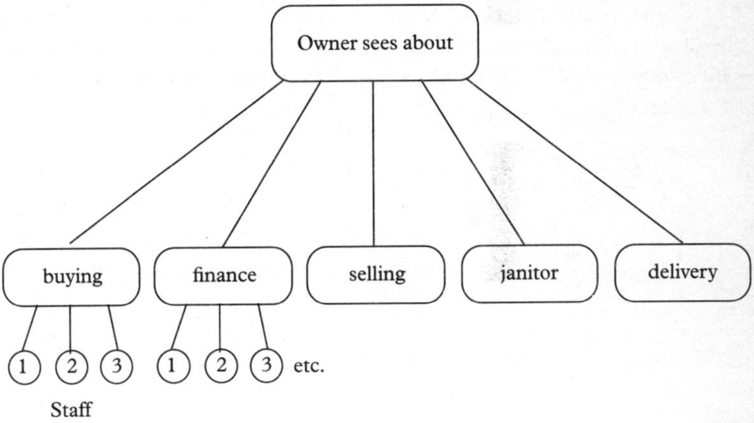

Figure 2.2 Diagram showing line organization

1. *Line organization structure* (Figure 2.2). In this method, authority is dispersed and delegated from top to bottom in a continuous line. The chief executive (or owner) will delegate authority to a number of departmental managers, who will in turn delegate to the individual members of staff under them. This form of organization is particularly suitable for a small business. Its other advantages are:

(a) It is very easy to understand.
(b) There is no doubt over who is to report to whom.
(c) Quick decisions are reached.
(d) Control and discipline are very simple to apply.
(e) It is very flexible and can be quickly adjusted to changing situations.

It is, however, difficult to fit into this type of structure the trained specialist whose services are required by more than one department. It tends also to be less suitable for larger firms.

2. *Staff organization structure* (Figure 2.3, opposite). This is a development of the line organization, to which are added a number of service departments – such as personnel and legal services – to provide specialized assistance to the main operating departments. (The word 'staff' is used in a special sense; it derives from army practice, where the officers in charge of back-up services such as supply and training are known as 'staff officers'.) The main advantage of this system is that it is easier to employ specialized personnel. The main disadvantage is that responsibility and authority are less clear-cut and disputes may arise between the specialist 'staff' personnel and heads of operating departments.
3. *Functional organizational structure* (Figure 2.4, page 26). This is one in which there are a number of specialists whose function is to supervise and control different aspects of the work of junior staff members. The subordinate takes orders from all the specialists and is accountable to them for particular aspects of his or her work. This form of organization needs a lot of commonsense and give and take if it is to work satisfactorily without a lot of arguments.

Organization charts

An organization chart is a presentation in pictorial form of the structure of an organization. It should also show the relationship between the personnel and the organization. The advantages of drawing such charts are:

1. They make managers think clearly about the best form of organization.
2. They define authority and help in drawing up job specifications.
3. They provide a visual aid for all concerned.
4. They give a clear idea of responsibility.
5. They prevent 'passing the buck' from one department to another.

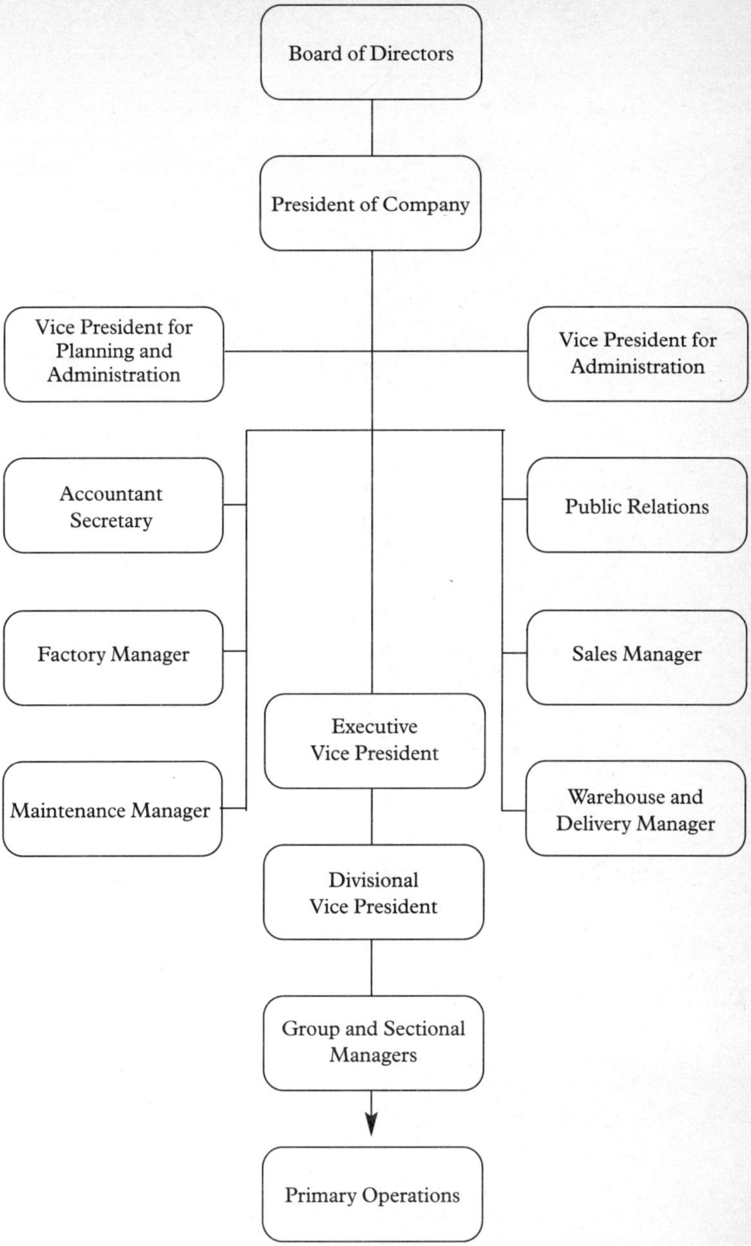

Figure 2.3 Diagram showing staff organization

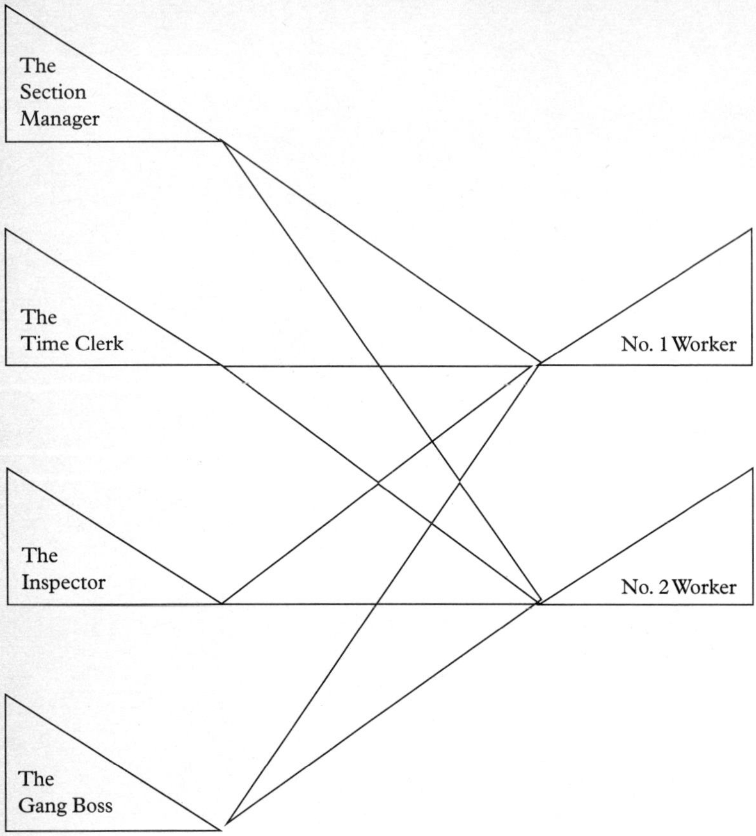

Figure 2.4 Diagram showing functional organization

The disadvantages are:

1. They may create dissatisfaction among those who think their status is too low.
2. They may represent the organization as the managers think it is, or as they would like it to be, and not as it really is.
3. They may get out of date unless frequently reviewed. There are three main methods of presenting organization charts – the vertical, horizontal and circular methods. These are shown in Figures 2.5 to 2.7. The vertical method is the most popular.

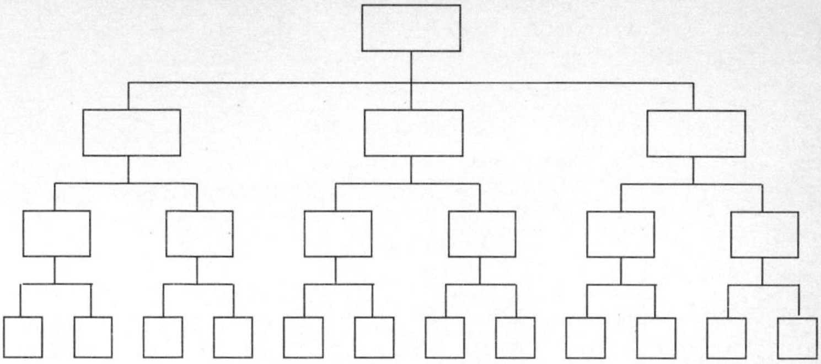

Figure 2.5 A vertical organization chart

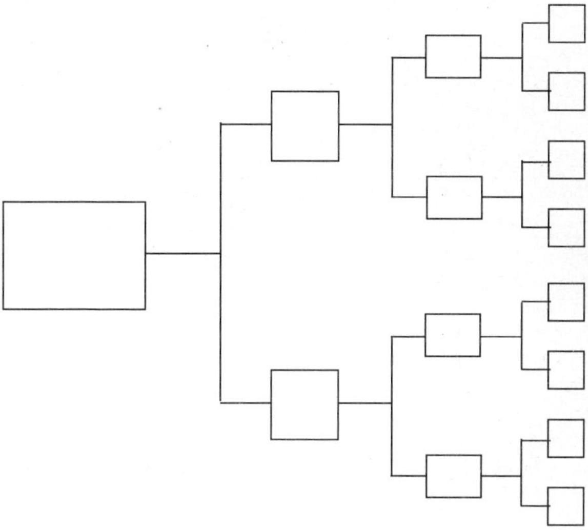

Figure 2.6 A horizontal organization chart

Rules for drawing and interpreting organization charts

1. If possible, all boxes at the same level of authority should be of the same size.
2. Positions of the same level of seniority should be on the same level on the chart.
3. Charts should be fully labelled, and dated.
4. Direct lines of responsibility should be shown by continuous lines; the main relations or points of contact between one department and another are shown by broken lines.

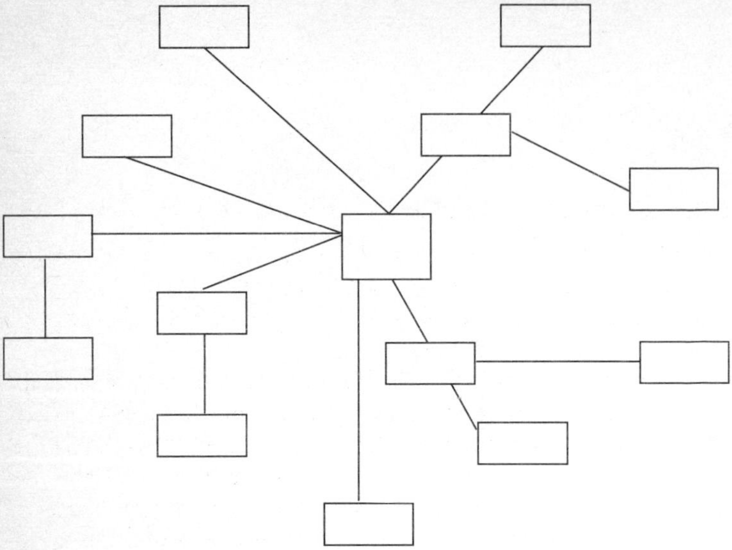

Figure 2.7 A circular organization chart

5. Charts should be regularly reviewed.
6. In large organizations, it may be impossible to show the full structure on one chart of reasonable size. In this case one general chart may be drawn showing the overall structure and separate, detailed charts showing the structure of each department.
7. Charts should be neatly drawn in black or dark blue ink, for ease of copying.

Effects of growth on organizational structure

An organization should always be changing to meet changing circumstances. This may mean changes in organizational structure. As seen above, a system suitable for a small firm may not be so good for a large one.

The usual effects of growth on organizational structure are:

1. The number of departments increases. There is more *delegation.*
2. More specialists can be employed.
3. More people need to be employed simply to look after or control other employees; the proportion of staff doing productive work tends to decline, thus tending to offset the advantages of scale.
4. There may be 'growing pains': some departments' work may increase greatly before extra staff can be recruited.

Generally, large businesses are more difficult to control than small ones. Difficulties may occur if one man (say the managing director) tries to control too many details and has too many subordinates reporting directly to him; if, in other words, he exceeds his span of control.

Management information systems: what are they?

Perhaps the best answer was given in 1981 by David M. Kroenke. It is interesting to note that although his reference was specifically to business computer systems, his definition can fit with any information system.

A system, he says, is a collection of various components that interact with each other to achieve a particular purpose. A computer system is a collection of various components (and this includes a computer) that interact to achieve a particular purpose. Take careful note that a computer system is not just the processing element. The computer is just one of the components. The other components are hardware, software or program (note the spelling), data, procedure and people. Each of these components is important and each one is needed to satisfy the business. If any one is taken away the business requirements cannot be satisfied.

The benefits of MIS in business

The Management Information System is designed to provide whatever information (on stock, sales, accounts, margins, etc.) the managers require in order to make informed decisions. Thus the benefits which result are:

1. Savings in time, money and labour.
2. Improvements in production and techniques in marketing.
3. Increased profits.
4. Increased competitiveness.

RESEARCH ACTIVITIES

Collect copies of any company documents you can: annual reports and accounts, partnership deeds, share certificates, etc. Make an exhibition of company documents.

Prepare an organization chart for a local business.

OR

Make a survey of the businesses in your town or country. State which ones are private, public or nationalized industries, and which are sole traders, partnerships, companies etc.

GROUP ACTIVITY

Working as a group, set up a company, and make a Memorandum of Association.

The title of your document is Memorandum of Association.

You should then write:

- the name of your company;
- the address of the Registered Office of your company;
- the objects of your company, saying what it does (e.g. runs a music shop);
- a Mission Statement;
- the statement that the liability of your members is limited;
- how much capital your company is registered with. This will consist of shares;
- what type of shares (see pages 14–15) your capital consists of.

Add an Association clause, signed by at least two members of the company, saying the number of shares they will each take.

SELF-REVISION QUESTIONS

1. List the characteristics of a sole trader. Which types of business are most suitable for him to operate?
2. Explain the main differences between a partnership and a limited company. What are the main advantages and disadvantages of each?
3. What is meant by limited liability? Which types of business may benefit from it? What are its possible harmful effects?
4. List the stages in the formation of a private company.
5. Say what is meant by the following terms:
   (a) certificate of trading;
   (b) ordinary share;
   (c) preference share;
   (d) cumulative preference share;

(e) debenture;
(f) dividend.

6. Define a nationalized industry. How does it differ from a government department?
7. Find out the nationalized industries which operate in your country and in each case state the name of the government minister responsible for supervising that industry.
8. Distinguish between the following:
   (a) Memorandum of association and articles of association.
   (b) Authorized and issued share capital.
   (c) Public and private companies.
9. What is the difference between producers' and consumers' co-operatives? Find out if there are examples of either type operating in your country.
10. Do you think that further industries should be nationalized? If so, which ones would you choose? (Give reasons.)
11. Find out the name of the government department or local authority which is responsible for each of the following in your area:
   (a) The police.
   (b) Street lighting.
   (c) Helping those who are out of a job.
   (d) Water supply.
   (e) Mending the roads.
12. Would you be in favour of further nationalization in your country? Give reasons.
13. What happens when a nationalized industry loses money? How does this differ from the situation in private industry?
14. What changes do you think a small shopkeeper might want to make in his organization if he opens another shop in a town 25km away?
15. What is meant by marketing? What activities carried out by the following could be described as marketing:
   (a) A shopkeeper.
   (b) A farmer.
   (c) A detergent manufacturer.
   (d) A large bank.
16. Draw up a simple organization chart for your school or college.

17. The ABC Co. Ltd has an authorized share capital of 200,000 ordinary shares of 50¢ each and 100,000 \$1 7½% preference shares. Three-quarters of the ordinary shares and half the preference shares have been issued and fully paid.
    (a) What is the total value of its:
        (i) Authorized share capital.
        (ii) Issued share capital.
        (iii) Paid-up share capital.
    (b) If in its first year it makes a profit of \$15,000, what is the maximum sum that will be available for distribution among its ordinary shareholders? (Remember: only half the preference shares have been issued.)
    (c) How much more capital will it raise by issuing all its remaining shares?
18. Explain the difference between the nominal value and market value of a share. Under what circumstances will the market value be higher than the nominal value?

3

Management and industrial relations

The task of the manager can be very varied; it needs intelligence, courage, hard work and original thinking, and the readiness to accept responsibility – this last quality being summed up in the word 'initiative'. A manager's work is therefore difficult to describe in words, but it will involve seven main elements:

1. *Planning.* Every new job must be planned, from building a factory to taking a journey. *All* the main steps must be thought out, placed in their correct order, and the best means of tackling them found.
2. *Organization.* This has two aspects. First, the workforce, materials and money necessary to put the plan into operation must be obtained and deployed in the right way, at the right time and in the right place. Second, a system must be set up (an organization structure) which will carry out routine tasks quickly, cheaply and efficiently.
3. *Direction.* Making sure everybody knows what they have to do and, if necessary, telling them how to do it.
4. *Control.* Someone who is having a house built does not go on a six-months holiday and expect the builder to get on with it; the owner or architect checks progress regularly and sees that everything has been done properly. A teacher gives her class exercises to make sure that it has understood its lessons. These are both examples of control, an essential management function.

   It is sometimes thought that checking up (or *supervision*) means that the manager does not trust the worker to do the job properly. This is not necessarily so. Although good supervision will detect slackness and dishonesty, it may also reveal that the original plan needs changing, that machinery needs repair, etc. It is also an opportunity for subordinates to discuss problems with management, and often suggest better working methods.
5. *Co-ordination.* A business of any size is split up for convenience into different sections or departments. Each has its job to do, but they

must all work together within the overall plan of the organization. Lack of this co-ordination is a frequent cause of inefficiency: one manager may quarrel with another; work may pile up on passing from one section to another; one group may stand idle because the previous group has fallen behind – and so on.

6. *Delegation.* There is a limit to what any one man or woman can do. When that limit is reached, the manager must delegate, i.e. let those lower down do some of his work and take some of the decisions. Delegation is not only necessary for efficiency; it is also a good means of training future managers and of improving morale.
7. *Motivation.* Why do some people work hard, while others slack off as soon as the boss's back is turned? No one has yet found a complete answer to this question. But we know that most people work better if they are well nourished, have adequate rest breaks, good working conditions and good pay. Sometimes other factors are considered important, such as an interesting job, an incentive bonus scheme for increased output, or the prospect of passing an examination or getting promotion. If a worker responds favourably to any of these factors, he is said to be well motivated; thus it is one of the manager's tasks to improve the workers' motivation.

   An old-fashioned form of motivation was fear of the sack. But few modern managers think that fear is an effective way of getting the best out of people; and trade unions and labour shortages take much of the sting out of such threats.

The manager's responsibility to the owners

In a business the owners – whether a sole proprietor, partners or shareholders – provide the capital needed to run the business. They expect a return on their investment equal to, or better than, they could obtain elsewhere by putting their money into other stocks and shares or by lending it to a bank. If a profit is made, capital can be increased and everyone is more inclined to invest more money in the business when this is needed for expansion. If a loss is made, capital is reduced; if losses are severe, or continue for any time, the capital can be all used up and the business becomes insolvent and comes to an end. The manager's over-riding responsibility, therefore, is to make a profit. In a competitive environment, this can only be done by maximizing income and keeping costs down – in short, by running the business efficiently.

It is sometimes thought that nationalized industries, government departments and local authorities do not need to be efficient because 'the government will always pay'. This is not the case. Large deficits have to be made up from increased taxation, and in any democratic country there is a limit to what the people are prepared to tolerate. In the end, any inefficient organization must be reorganized, trimmed or even closed down altogether.

The manager is responsible for other people's money. Proper accounts must therefore be kept to make sure that this money is being correctly used and safeguarded. The manager must also provide the owners with agreed financial and other information necessary for overall control of the business by the proprietors. For example, companies must publish their accounts and produce an annual report; these are sent every year to all shareholders before the annual general meeting at which they must be approved. Similar reports are produced by nationalized industries and other bodies handling public money; where necessary they are discussed and approved by Parliament.

The manager's responsibility to employees

Until recent years, the law only recognized the manager's responsibility to the owners, or providers of capital. Labour was simply a commodity to be hired at the cheapest possible rate, and worked as hard as possible. Now the rights of workers are also recognized, as are those of their representatives, the trade unions. The legal position differs from one country to another, but the following responsibilities of a business towards its employees are usually recognized:

1. *Fair wages.* Where trade unions are not strong enough to negotiate good wages, minimum rates of pay are often laid down by law. Wages must also be paid in cash, not in goods or vouchers.
2. *Protection against unfair dismissal.* This is a more recent concept, and still far from universal. Where it exists, the worker may be able to take the employer to court and claim compensation if he thinks he has been unfairly dismissed.
3. *Safe working conditions.* A mass of laws and regulations has grown up, governing the way that factories and other dangerous places of work should be run. They prescribe such things as:
   (a) Guarding of dangerous machinery.
   (b) Regular inspections of machinery and installations generally.
   (c) Protective clothing and goggles.
   (d) Adequate ventilation.
   (e) First-aid facilities.
   (f) Regular medical check-ups for those handling dangerous or poisonous substances.
4. *Compensation for industrial injuries.* Employers are usually obliged to take out insurance against these, just as motorists are compelled to take out third-party insurance on their cars.

5. *Non-discrimination.* Employers may be fined if they discriminate against certain classes of workers, such as trade union members.
6. *Protection for women and children.* The law may state that certain types of work may not be done by women or children, and the hours that they work are often strictly limited.
7. *Proper training* for the job, often wholly or partly at the employer's expense.

The manager's responsibility to customers

This is often referred to as *consumer protection.* It has become much more important recently. It can be summed up as the responsibility to provide safe, good-quality merchandise to the public in a way which does not mislead the public as to its true nature. The way that this is carried out is described in Chapters 4 and 7 under the headings 'Contracts affecting the consumer' and 'Consumer protection' respectively.

A business is also responsible in law for any injury suffered by customers legitimately on its premises. If for example a housewife trips over a step or carelessly-placed carton in a shop, then the shopkeeper may be responsible for damages.

The manager's responsibility to society

In the nineteenth century, the famous English law case of Rylands v. Fletcher established the principle that, if a man keeps an inherently dangerous substance or animal on his property, and it escapes, then he is responsible for the damage it causes, whether or not he has been negligent. Since then this legal protection has been greatly extended in most countries to cover the possible damage to the environment caused by factories, mines, etc.

This protection is vital to the community, even if it increases the cost of production. Consider some of the things that can occur if industry does not exercise proper care:

1. Smoke and dangerous chemicals can pollute the atmosphere. This often damages crops and makes people and animals ill.
2. Chemicals or untreated sewage escaping into rivers will kill fish and make it impossible to use the water for drinking.
3. Factories, rubbish tips or quarries in the wrong place can turn pleasant countryside into an eyesore. This can ruin tourism as well as the pleasure of the local inhabitants.
4. Careless farming, burning of brush or tree-felling can lead to soil erosion and flooding.

5. Underground mining, if carelessly carried out, can lead to dangerous mineshafts or collapse of buildings above.
6. Inadequately fenced or protected factories, building works or quarries can be a danger to the public, particularly children.
7. Water needs to be conserved, particularly where there is a long dry season. Many industrial processes use a lot of water, but changes in working methods may lead to savings.
8. Recycling materials means using them again, perhaps in the same way, perhaps in a different way. This has two advantages. One is that it avoids wasting valuable raw materials (for example recycling paper means using fewer trees to make new paper). The other is that it reduces the amount of waste which has to be disposed of.
9. Packaging may involve a great deal of waste. Businesses may also have a choice whether to use disposable containers etc., or ones which may be cleaned and used again. Food and drink are good examples of this.

Management may also provide a service to society, by sponsorship, by community service, and by giving employment and training in a responsible way.

Leadership

Leadership has been described as the goal-directed motivation of people. A leader is willing and able to accept the responsibility of leading a group of people to accomplish a certain objective. It is still not fully understood why some people are 'born' leaders, others can learn the art, while many people can never do so. The owner or managers of a business should always look out for people who can be promoted to positions of leadership and responsibility. This can be at any level, from the foreman of a small group of workers to a departmental head, responsible for the work of many dozens of men and women.

Good leaders are very important in all organizations. Under a good leader people will work willingly and well; under a poor leader (usually a person who has been promoted to a position of responsibility without the ability to do the job), matters will drift, people will be discontented, and muddle and confusion will reign. It is important to note that, to be effective, a leader must not only be properly appointed (whether by the managing director of a company, or by democratic vote in a club or society); his leadership must also be accepted by those he is to lead. Sometimes a leader is chosen because he is recognized as 'the best man for the job'. Sometimes, however, the so-called 'hereditary' principle is used. In the old days, it was always assumed that a king would be succeeded by his eldest son; this principle is still used today when the proprietor hands on his business to his son, or a man is promoted to a post because of long service in the organization.

There are four basic styles of leadership:

1. *Authoritarian.* The leader decides what to do and it is done, whatever others may think.
2. *Participative or democratic.* Those likely to be affected by a decision are consulted before the decision is made (although sometimes the leader reserves the right not to accept the majority view). This allows those lower down to become involved and interested in policy, but it tends to slow down decision-making and is expensive in staff time.
3. *Laissez-faire.* This is French for 'let them do it'. It means in this context that the leader deliberately stands back and lets the subordinates plan their own work and take their own decisions as far as possible.
4. *Charismatic.* A charismatic leader is one who is able to lead simply by reason of his or her outstanding personality or character, i.e. their charisma. Some great managers, politicians and generals have been able to break all the normal rules and yet succeed, simply because of their outstanding charisma.

A leader may combine any of these styles as circumstances dictate.

Labour relations

Some industries, and some firms within industries, have a history of labour disputes, strikes and go-slows. Others go for years on end without any trouble. Why is this? No one has the complete answer, but the following are frequent causes of labour unrest.

1. Low pay – particularly if the workers believe that less skilled men are earning more elsewhere.
2. Bad working conditions.
3. Monotonous work, or irregular hours.
4. Bad management – especially failure to tackle long-standing grievances.
5. Delay in getting an answer to workers' or unions' requests.
6. Unsettled employment prospects.
7. Inconsistent enforcement of rules and regulations; for example, a 'No smoking' rule may be widely ignored, followed by a sudden

'clamp-down' on employees, who then think that they are being victimized.
8. Existence of a few 'trouble-makers' on the staff.
9. 'Who-does-what' disputes between one group of workers and another, or between one union and another.

Good labour relations demand hard work, and often long negotiations. Wise managers will try to avoid the situations listed above, although some (particularly No. 3) may be impossible to remove.

Many firms agree a *grievance procedure* with their workers. This is a series of steps to be taken if a worker or group of workers has a complaint about their pay or conditions of work. A grievance procedure will not, by itself, guarantee good labour relations, since management may contest the claim, but it should prevent minor difficulties being blown up into major unrest or strikes.

Trade unions

A trade union is an association of workers in an industry or group of industries. The object of all trade unions is to improve the wages and working conditions of their members; they also help individual members who are in trouble with their employers. They arose in the nineteenth century when it was realized that the individual worker, on his own, was in a poor bargaining position, but that if all the workers acted together they were in a much stronger bargaining position to win concessions from the management. The motto of the trade union movement is therefore 'In unity is strength'.

Today trade unions are accepted as an important part of industrial life in all democratic countries. The ways in which they seek to improve the conditions of their members are very varied, but the most important are:

1. By organizing the workers, that is:
   (a) Encouraging as many as possible to join the union.
   (b) Ensuring proper organization of branches.
   (c) Making certain that their policies reflect the feelings of the workers.
   (d) Encouraging all members to act together to achieve common aims.
2. Negotiating improved pay and conditions with the management, which may include shorter working hours, longer holidays or better overtime payments.
3. Protecting workers against unhealthy or dangerous working conditions.

4. Protecting workers against unfair dismissal.
5. Calling workers out on strike if concessions cannot be obtained by negotiation. (Responsible unions will only call a strike as a last resort, since the workers get no wages during the strike and the union may have to give them strike pay.)
6. Educating workers in trade union practices through lectures, pamphlets and courses.
7. Representing the workers' point of view to government when new laws or tax changes are proposed, and getting better social security.
8. Discussing with the government and employers' associations the state of the economy and the ways in which prosperity can be increased.
9. Providing sick pay and unemployment insurance schemes for their members, if government provisions are inadequate.

In some countries trade unions have been much more successful than in others. The following points should be noted when comparing one union with another, or one country's unions with another:

1. The ability of the union to negotiate and represent the workers depends on its strength, its membership, its organization and the skill of its officers in negotiation.
2. There may be more than one union representing workers in a particular industry.
3. Trade union officials should bear in mind that increased wages in the long term can only come from an increase in productivity; increased wages in the short term can result in inflation, or in weakening the employer's profit or competitive position so much that he or she has to dismiss workers or even close the business down.
4. There is bound to be government intervention at some time, particularly over the following matters:
   (a) Legislation for minimum wages.
   (b) Arbitration in case of deadlock in negotiations. In Trinidad, trade disputes are referred, where necessary, to the Industrial Court or to the Minister of Labour.
   (c) Prohibition of strikes in certain industries.
   (d) Protection of unions against being sued by employers for loss of profits during a strike.

There are different types of union, classified according to the type of worker they represent:

1. *Industrial unions* – representing workers in a particular industry such as the oil industry or the sugar industry.

2. *General unions* – representing workers (usually unskilled or semi-skilled) not connected to any industry but mostly in direct services such as transport or catering.
3. *Craft unions* – representing highly skilled workers such as engineers or draftsmen; membership is usually restricted to those with agreed qualifications.
4. *White-collar unions* – representing those such as teachers, clerks or government officials.
5. *Social unions* – representing people such as entertainers, steelband men and calypsonians. (This is not really a trade union as such.)

As an indication of their numbers and variety, some of the trade unions in Trinidad and Tobago are: the Oilfields Workers' Trade Union; Public Services Association; Trinidad and Tobago Unified Teachers' Association; Transport and Industrial Workers' Union; Aviation Communication and Allied Workers' Union; Communication Workers' Union; Postmen's Union; Police Services Association; Fire Services Association; Prison Services Association; All Trinidad Sugar Estates and General Workers' Union; Islandwide Cane Farmers' Trade Union; National Foodcrop Farmers' Association; Steel Workers' Association of Trinidad and Tobago; Bank and General Workers' Union; and the Sugar Industry Staff Association.

Wages and payment systems

It is a well-known fact that some workers earn more than others. This is true even in communist countries. The main reason for this is that some workers, because of their ability or better training, are better able to meet the needs of society at a given time than others. However, the difference (or *differential*) between the highest and the lowest paid varies greatly from one country to another. The factors influencing this are very complicated, but some of the most important are:

1. The type of economy – differentials tend to be higher in an economy that leans towards the free market pattern than in a controlled or socialist economy.
2. The degree of prosperity – lower-paid workers tend to be better off in prosperous countries (where there is often a labour shortage) than in poor or under-developed countries (where there is often high unemployment).
3. The relative strength of the unions or professional associations representing the different types of worker – the general unions will try to reduce differentials, while craft and white-collar unions will try to increase them.

4. Demand and supply – if a particular skill is in short supply, those who have it are in a strong position to negotiate higher wages.
5. Government policy – this is particularly important in deciding the wage rates of the different types of worker employed by the government and in nationalized industries.

Workers with long service may receive higher wages than beginners. Wage rates may also be higher in the towns than in the country. It may also be necessary to pay higher wages to attract workers into dirty, dangerous or unpleasant jobs.

There are several different systems for calculating wages and salaries:

1. *Straight salary.* The worker receives a salary of so many dollars per month or per year, in return for a minimum period of work each week. No overtime is paid for work over this minimum. This is the usual method of remuneration for teachers, managers and senior office workers and civil servants.
2. *Time wages or day rate.* The worker is paid so much per hour or per day or per week. If the hours worked per day exceed a stipulated number (usually seven or eight), extra hours are paid at higher (*overtime*) rates. This is the most common method of payment for manual and clerical workers, and it is the only system possible where output is difficult to measure, or where quality of work is more important than quantity.
3. *Piece work.* The worker is paid so much for each piece or item produced. He is thus encouraged to work harder and faster, but there is always a danger of skimped or sub-standard work. He may also suffer (for no fault of his own) if the supply of work is interrupted by strikes or breakdowns. In practice, piece-work systems are often combined with a small time payment.
4. *Bonus systems.* These were invented as an improvement on piece work. Work study engineers calculate a worker's 'normal' daily or weekly output. This may involve long negotiations with his trade union. If his output is below the norm, he receives only a time payment, but if it is above the norm, he receives in addition a *bonus* depending on the number of extra items produced or the time saved. For example, under the Halsey system the bonus might be worked out as follows:

Time allowed:	200 hours (to produce given output)
Time taken:	160 hours
Hourly rate:	$3.00
Premium bonus:	50% of time saved

Time taken × hourly rate	= 160 hours × $3 =	$480
Saving on time	= 40 hours × $3 =	$120
Add Bonus	= 50% × $120 =	$60
Total payment for 160 hours' work		$540

(equivalent to hourly rate of $3.375 instead of normal $3)

5. *Gang bonus system.* The bonus is based on the total output of the gang or factory and shared out among all the workers, usually in proportion to their hourly rates of pay.
6. *Profit-sharing.* This is rare, but is sometimes employed by fishermen, who may receive no wages but a share of the profit from the sale of their catch.
7. *Stint system.* The worker is allowed to go home on completion of a prescribed job.
8. *Tips or service charges.* Hotel and restaurant workers in particular rely on tips from customers for a large part of their income. The modern trend is for tips to be replaced by a service charge which is added to the customer's bill and then shared out among the staff by the management, in addition to their regular wages.

Co-operation

Co-operation, or teamwork, is vital if an organization is to run efficiently. If Miss A is always quarrelling with Mrs B, or won't speak to Mr C, or if Mr D never gets round to looking over some vital document – then the whole work of an office can be held up. Such childish behaviour must be stamped on firmly by management at an early stage. If this fails to cure the trouble, then the person responsible should be moved to another department or asked to find work elsewhere.

In industry, such co-operation is even more important. Its failure can lead to lack of work and loss of earnings for other workers. It can also lead to danger. It is necessary for all those in an organization to understand their part in the total operation; that is to say, their role is not merely to do their own job efficiently, it is also to do their utmost to achieve the aims of the organization as a whole.

Effective communication

No one can function efficiently if they are not told what to do (or, at a higher level, not kept fully in the picture). The way that vital information is transmitted through an organization is through its *communications system.* Every organization has one; though if it is allowed to grow up without proper thought, it will not be very efficient, because vital information will not get through, and it will rely too much on gossip and rumour.

The main means of communication are:

1. *Word of mouth, usually face-to-face.* The managing director gives information in a meeting to the departmental managers, who then inform their foremen, who then inform their workers. Obviously this cannot be used for very complicated instructions, but it is an important channel of communication, particularly where persuasion or co-operation is involved, since it maintains vital person-to-person contact.
2. *Telephone* (internal or external systems). A quick and easy means of communication with specific people, but not everyone can be reached by phone, and important messages need to be confirmed in writing.
3. *Letters, memos and forms.* Usually delivered by messengers based in the firm's post room. Forms are particularly efficient at conveying routine, standardized information, but there is always a risk of unnecessary proliferation.
4. *Notice boards and public address systems.* Useful for giving simple information to large numbers of people. Cannot be used for anything confidential.
5. *House magazines and newsletters.* Expensive to compile and print, but very large firms may find them useful as a means of keeping scattered branches in touch with what is going on elsewhere in the organization.
6. *Circulars.* Sometimes placed in wage packets. Should be reserved for information which it is essential that all employees have in writing.
7. *Instruction manuals.* For technical information.
8. *Data terminals and print-outs.* Used where information is stored on a computer, such as customers' account details or monthly sales by item.
9. *Fax, e-mail, internet, ISDN.*

Having established an efficient means of getting information to his or her employees, the wise manager will also encourage the flow of relevant information back from the employees. (The word 'relevant' needs to be stressed, since he can all too easily be flooded with papers which he never has time to read.) This will consist not only of data and statistics necessary for managerial decision-making, but also 'feedback'. This is a general term covering staff and customers' reaction to the firm, its policies and its products. It is vital to know what is going on throughout the organization, and the manager should encourage those directly involved to tell him. This will supplement his own observation and questions.

There are three main means by which feedback can be organized. Many organizations use them all.

1. *Regular reports,* to be submitted at specified intervals (e.g. once a month).
2. *Exception reports,* submitted only when a specified event occurs (or fails to occur) – for example, a machine breakdown or item running out of stock.
3. *Suggestion schemes,* designed so that all ideas occurring to employees are exploited, or at least considered. These may be organized via departmental heads, or suggestion boxes into which workers can 'post' their suggestions.

Here is a sample format for a report:

i. Title of report.
ii. Terms of reference.
iii. Procedure.
iv. Findings.
v. Conclusion.
vi. Recommendations.
vii. Signature of report-writer and date.

These can be supplemented by meetings and consultative committees, but these use up a lot of staff and management time, and the benefit gained must be weighed against the cost.

ACTIVITIES

1. Find out all you can about recycling in the home and in business. Look at what is thrown away. Could this be re-used? Could something permanent (e.g. proper plates, cups) be used instead? Could the things which are thrown away be used for something else, or recycled? Is there any way in which your local government or businesses try to recover and recycle materials (e.g. bottle banks, can banks)? Can you suggest ways in which your school or college can recycle or avoid waste?
2. Find out the names of trade unions in your country. Make a list of them and say what type of worker they represent (see pages 39–41).

SELF-REVISION QUESTIONS

1. Why is management necessary?
2. What is the difference between management and leadership? Can the one exist without the other?
3. List the seven main elements of the management task. Illustrate their application by reference to an organization known to you, such as a football team.
4. Some employees resent close supervision of their work. Discuss whether you think such resentment is justified.
5. What is initiative? Give an example.
6. State, with reason, which of the following statements you think are correct:
   (a) Managers delegate work to train their subordinates.
   (b) Managers delegate work which they do not want to do themselves.
   (c) Managers delegate work to give themselves more time for other matters.
   (d) Managers delegate work which they cannot do themselves.
7. Imagine that you have a younger brother or sister who, in your opinion, is not doing enough work for a forthcoming examination. How would you motivate him or her to work harder?
8. List the responsibilities of management to the providers of capital.
9. Do the responsibilities you have described in Question 8 conflict with those of management to the employees?
10. Find out what legal protection of workers' rights exists in your country.
11. Do you consider that business has other responsibilities to society beyond those listed in this chapter?
12. What is meant by participative leadership?
13. Why is a leader followed and obeyed?
14. Which factors are most important in good labour relations?
15. Do you think that trade unions help or hinder the economic development of your country?
16. What are differentials? What are the factors that increase or decrease them?
17. Explain the difference between the piece work and bonus system. Why is piece work sometimes considered unsatisfactory?
18. What factors, besides pay, contribute to making a worker satisfied with his or her job?

19. Which means of communication would you recommend in a large factory for the following:
    (a) A message about revised wage rates to departmental managers.
    (b) An announcement about revised bus schedules to and from the works.
    (c) An announcement about a badly parked car causing obstruction.
    (d) A complaint from a worker about dangerous machinery.
20. Find out what *minutes* are in business and then explain the significance of the saying that committees take minutes and waste hours.

4

Legal aspects of business: contracts

Essentials of a valid contract

A contract is an agreement which can be enforced at law. Hundreds (if not thousands) of contracts are made every day – a contract is made every time a business transaction takes place. Thus the law of contract is at the heart of business activity.

An agreement becomes a contract only if *all six* of the following conditions are satisfied:

1. There must be an *offer* by one person and *acceptance* of the offer by another. An offer can be withdrawn at any time before it is accepted, but not afterwards.
2. The persons entering into the agreement must both have the *capacity* to do so. Those whose capacity is limited include:
   (a) Children.
   (b) Those under the influence of drink or drugs.
   (c) Lunatics.
   (d) Public bodies (if acting *ultra vires,* i.e. beyond the powers given them by law) and limited companies (if doing things not covered by their objects clause).
3. There must be no *force, fraud* or *misrepresentation.*
4. The thing contemplated must be *legal.*
5. There must be *consideration.* This means that if one party agrees to provide goods or services, something of value must be given in exchange. This may be money, or other goods or services; it may also consist of forbearance, e.g. agreement not to press another legal claim; but it does *not* cover agreeing to do something one is legally obliged to do anyway. Consideration need not be at a realistic commercial value to be valid.
6. Contracts must be *certain* – that is, specific (certain) as regards which parties are involved, the price, and the subject matter (e.g. the goods) involved.

Some important points should be noted:

1. Most contracts need not be in writing to be valid (the major exceptions to this rule are noted in the next section). In fact most contracts are made by word of mouth. If you take a taxi down town, then you make a contract with the taxi-driver; he agrees to take you to your destination, and in return you agree by implication (see below) to pay the fare. Once the offer has been accepted, the contract is made. Obviously, if it is important or complicated, the terms should be set out as soon as possible in a *memorandum of agreement*, signed by both parties, to prevent disputes later.
2. A mere promise (an agreement to do something without consideration in return) is not legally enforceable, unless made in writing with special legal formalities called *writing under seal.*
3. *Implied conditions* may be made part of the contract. These are unwritten (or unmentioned) terms and rules which the courts will assume that you have accepted, unless specific agreement has been made to the contrary. For instance, if you step on a bus, it is implied that you have agreed to pay the fare and agreed to abide by the rules (or conditions of carriage) of the bus company. If you go into a hotel and order a drink, you have by implication agreed to pay whatever they like to charge you for it, unless you agreed the price beforehand. It is no defence to claim later that the price is exorbitant.
4. An offer must be accepted exactly as it is made to form a valid contract. If X says to Y 'I will sell you this watch for $20' and Y replies 'OK, if you will have it cleaned first', then Y's reply is not an acceptance, but a *counter-offer.* Only if X accepts this new offer is a contract made.

Agreements which fail to satisfy the six rules above are said to be *void.* They can never be legally enforced. A *voidable* contract, on the other hand, can be set aside by the injured party, but if he chooses to treat it as binding, then he can still enforce it against the other party. Suppose, for example, that Vijay induces Krishna to make a contract with him by fraudulent misrepresentation – to sell his car to him by claiming falsely that it is unsafe to be on the road. Krishna can set aside the agreement, because it breaches rule (3) above, but as he made it in good faith, he can choose to continue it if he wishes, and oblige Vijay to honour it by paying for the car.

Contracts can be brought to an end *(discharged)* in the following circumstances:

1. By performance – both sides completing what they have agreed to do.

2. By the subject-matter ceasing to exist – if you agree to buy a dog which dies before you take possession of it, for example.
3. By death (though the dead person's debts must still be paid) or bankruptcy.
4. By notice – for example, a contract of employment can be ended by either party giving the agreed length of notice.
5. By mutual agreement, or substitution of a fresh agreement.
6. By lapse of time – if a time limit is part of the agreement.
7. By legislation – if something which was legal at the time it was agreed is made illegal before it can be performed.
8. By occurrence of any event which the parties have agreed would nullify the agreement if it occurred.

Specialty contracts

These are a special group of contracts which are not valid unless made in writing and *signed, sealed and delivered.* The first of these three terms needs no explanation, except that an illiterate person 'signs' by making his mark on the document before witnesses. Sealing is done either by a company or corporation impressing its common seal onto the document, or by a private citizen (who has no seal) signing in the presence of a notary public (in practice, usually a solicitor). Delivery means handing over to the other party; its significance is that a specialty contract does not become operative until this is done, whereas a simple contract becomes operative as soon as the offer has been accepted. Specialty contracts are also known as *deeds.*

The following contracts are of no legal effect unless made under seal:

1. Contracts made without consideration.
2. Conveyances of land, legal mortgages and leases for more than three years.
3. Transfer of shares in a company (which must bear the seal of the company concerned to be valid).

In addition, certain other contracts must be made in writing to be enforceable, although the law does not prescribe any particular form for some of them. They are:

1. Contracts of guarantee or suretyship (i.e. agreements to pay compensation in the event of a third party's default or misdemeanour).
2. Agreements to sell, lease or rent land.
3. Bills of exchange and promissory notes (this includes cheques).
4. Assignments of copyright.

5. Contracts of insurance.
6. Charter parties (agreements for hire of ships).
7. Hire-purchase agreements.

Readers may be puzzled to note land appearing under both headings. The explanation is that the *agreement to sell* (or lease or rent) needs only to be in writing to be legally enforceable – an exchange of letters would do – and this is the 'exchange of contracts' in house-purchase transactions. The *transfer of title,* however, or conveyance of legally recognized ownership, must be made under seal.

In some countries, contracts of employment and/or apprenticeship must be in writing. In most of the Caribbean, employment contracts for the banking service, the public service, teaching, and for many jobs in the private sector, are in writing, and set out clearly the conditions under which the worker is employed.

Contracts affecting the consumer

More and more, governments are realizing that the strict enforcement of the rules of contract outlined above may lead to injustice for the consumer. Unscrupulous traders may exploit ordinary citizens' ignorance of out-of-the-way aspects of the law; they may lead them to sign contracts which are weighted against them because they do not read the 'small print' (and would not understand it if they did); they may produce impressive-looking 'guarantees' which in fact imply acceptance of conditions which take away many of the purchaser's common-law rights. The law of contract grew up over the centuries on the assumption that the parties would have more or less equal bargaining power and either know the law well themselves or be able to afford a solicitor. This assumption still holds good as far as dealings between one business and another are concerned. But the ordinary citizen is at a disadvantage. So legislatures in certain states of the USA began to 'tilt the balance' in the consumer's favour, and countries elsewhere – including the Caribbean – have begun to follow suit.

In practice, consumer protection in contract has usually taken the following forms:

1. Strict control over hire-purchase transactions, to make sure that the hire purchaser knows what he is committed to before he signs.
2. Control over the conditions which traders – such as dry-cleaners and repair-men, who are responsible for the public's property while it is in their hands – can impose. For instance, the courts may refuse to accept as an implied condition of contract a notice such as 'No

responsibility accepted for damage, however caused', if it takes away the trader's common-law duty to take reasonable care of property entrusted to his charge.

3. Control over bogus guarantees and warranties.
4. Registration of moneylenders and brokers and prohibition of exorbitant rates of interest.
5. Strengthening of consumers' powers of redress over shoddy or dangerous goods. This includes sometimes *strict product liability,* an assumption that the manufacturer is responsible for any damage his goods may cause, whether or not he has been demonstrably negligent, and whether or not he has a direct contractual relationship with the victim.

These measures need to be accompanied by programmes of consumer education. Citizens cannot be expected to stand up for their rights unless they know what they are.

ACTIVITIES

Find as many contracts or agreements as you can. For example a hire-purchase agreement, a contract of employment, or the conditions on an airline ticket.

Find out what government controls over contracts of employment exist in your country. (Possible sources of information might include reference books, government pamphlets, Citizens' Advice Bureaux, trade unions.)

SELF-REVISION QUESTIONS

1. What is the difference between an agreement and a contract?
2. State the six essentials of a valid contract.
3. Explain the legal meaning of consideration.
4. Why is it desirable that contracts should be in writing?
5. Why is a promise not normally enforceable at law?
6. State what implied conditions might exist in the following circumstances:
   (a) Leaving a car in a garage for repair.
   (b Checking into a hotel.
   (c) Buying an airline ticket.
   (d) Buying an airline ticket with a credit card.

7. Explain the difference between a void and a voidable contract. Give two examples of each.
8. Under what circumstances can a contract be discharged?
9. A publisher makes an agreement with an author to write a book about a series of test matches, which is later cancelled. Does the contract still exist after the cancellation of the cricket matches?
10. Define a specialty contract.
11. List four types of contract which must be made in writing, and state whether each one is a specialty contract or not.
12. What is the common seal of a company? When is it used?
13. Say what reasons you think led governments to insist that hire-purchase contracts must be in writing, while ordinary contracts of sale need not be.
14. Is it unfair for the government to intervene in contracts made between business concerns and consumers?
15. What is meant by strict liability in law? Give an example of where it might apply, or where you think it ought to apply.

5

The factors of production

Adam Smith (whom we met in Chapter 1) was the first to identify the three essential *factors of production* without which production cannot take place. He called them *land, labour* and *capital.* We would also include *entrepreneurial,* or *management, skill.*

1. *Land.* This is perhaps better described as 'natural resources'. These include coal, oil, minerals, stone and other building materials, fertile soil (for growing crops in), growing timber, and fish in seas and rivers, even the water which we drink.
2. *Labour.* This describes all forms of work, of hand or brain, needed to transform natural resources into a form useful to man.
3. *Capital.* This is the money needed to buy the land, machinery and equipment needed – everything from a plough to an oil refinery – and to pay the workers who provide the labour.
4. *Entrepreneurial or management skill.* The factor which brings all the other three factors together into a profitable combination.

All these ingredients are essential to industry and commerce. Suppose, for example, that the inhabitants of a very small island discovered oil offshore. This is a valuable natural resource, but it will be of no use unless some means can be found to provide the capital to pay for all the very expensive extraction and refining equipment, and the labour to operate that machinery. Modern industry is very complex. In Adam Smith's day, the master or owner (who provided the capital) usually ran his own business, which was on a much smaller scale. Today large numbers of managers and administrators are needed, and the capital may be provided by large numbers of small shareholders or financial institutions who may not want to play any active part in running the business. In other words, capital and control have become divorced. For this reason, some writers add a fourth factor of production, *entrepreneurial* or *management skill* – that factor that brings the other three factors together into a profitable combination.

Natural resources of the Caribbean

All the islands of the Caribbean have forest reserves producing lumber for the home market. Guyana also exports lumber from her exceptionally large reserves. There are sand and gravel beds in all the islands used in road construction.

Country	*Resource*	*Location*
Jamaica	Bauxite	Manchester, Clarendon, St Elisabeth, St Catherine, St Anns.
	Gypsum	Bulls Bay near the capital.
	Selicia sand	St Elisabeth.
	Marble	Eastern Jamaica and the southern slopes of the Blue Mountains.
Trinidad and Tobago	Iron Ore	Northern Range.
	Asphalt	La Brea.
	Gypsum	Northern Range.
	Limestone	Central Trinidad.
	Sand and gravel	The mountain ranges, the rivers for gravel. Sand is found in the sand hills in central Trinidad.
	Oil	Off shore – Soladado and Galeota Fields. Inland – in the entire south of the island and in Tabaquite in central Trinidad.
	Natural gas	In close proximity to oil-producing areas.
Guyana	Bauxite	Junction of Alluvial belt, Peneplain – east of Essequibo River. Linden on Demerara River, Ituru and Kwakwani on the Berbice River.
	Diamonds	Upper Mazarini River, Border near Cuyuni River.
	Gold	Cuyuni River and Potaro River.
	Manganese	Matthew Ridge and Port Kaituma.
	Columbite	Interior. (These are used in the airplane industry.)
	Tantalite	
	Platinum	
Barbados	Natural gas	Around Rock Hall in the North.

Table 5.1 Natural resources of the Caribbean

Supply of labour

An industry can only function if it can obtain the right type and quantity of workers. The same is true of most types of commerce. The supply of labour, and ultimately a country's prosperity, depends on the following factors:

1. The total population of the country, which is affected by the birth rate – the number of children born every year, the age at which people die; the rate of immigration and emigration.
2. The part of the population which is available for employment; in many countries the proportion of children and old people is tending to increase.
3. The quality of the education and training available.
4. The adequacy and efficiency of the health and social services.
5. The attitude of the people towards work.
6. The transport available so that workers can get to and from work.
7. The rate of pay and the level of wages.
8. Religious and traditional attitudes.
9. The age to which children are kept at school.
10. The age at which people retire.
11. The mobility of labour – the extent to which people are prepared to move to new areas to find work. Mobility is the willingness to move; it is not the same thing as migration.
12. The number of women seeking employment; this will obviously be higher if there are a lot of well-paid jobs for them, or if they can find other people to look after their children.
13. The type of labour available; workers must be trained and able to do the jobs for which there are vacancies (e.g. a postman cannot be employed as a doctor).

From this it can be seen that the factors affecting the supply of labour can be very complex. The number of jobs available can also vary, and governments still find it very difficult to forecast demand and supply for labour accurately. When there are more workers than jobs, there is said to be *unemployment* (a worker able to work but without a job is unemployed). When there are more jobs than workers to do them, there is a *labour shortage*. Sometimes there is unemployment and a labour shortage at the same time. This is because those out of a job do not have the skills, or the educational qualifications, to fill the posts for which there are vacancies. Sometimes a worker can be retrained to do a new type of job, but this is a costly and lengthy process.

The types of employment can be classified as follows:

1. *Professional and scientific*. This covers those who need very high educational qualifications and have to take examinations to make sure that they will do their jobs with the necessary skill. It covers doctors,

accountants, lawyers, surveyors, engineers, research scientists and so on.

2. *Managerial.* These are people running their own businesses, or whose job it is to organize the work of others.
3. *Supervisory.* These people, such as foremen, inspectors, etc., who supervise or control the work of others.
4. *Clerical and secretarial.* These are the book-keepers, secretaries, etc. who work in offices. They are sometimes called 'white-collar' workers, from the time when male clerks were expected to wear a stiff white collar at work.
5. *Skilled manual workers and technicians.* This covers those who have undergone an apprenticeship or other extensive training – motor mechanics, repairmen, electricians, etc.
6. *Semi-skilled workers.* Those who need some training and experience but can learn the job fairly quickly.
7. *Unskilled workers.* People who need no training to do the job – cleaners, porters, building labourers, etc.

As more and more machinery and computers are used, the demand for unskilled labour is tending to diminish, but there is greater demand for professional people and skilled workers. All countries in the Caribbean are making great efforts to train and produce as many of these people as possible.

Unemployment, too, can be classified into types:

1. *Seasonal.* The sugar cane cutters, for example, work only part of the year, so they may be unemployed the rest of the time.
2. *Structural.* When there is a change in the amount of demand for a particular *type of* product, the employment level *will also* change.
3. *Cyclical.* This *type* of unemployment is a reflection of the normal trade cycle of boom and depression (see Chapter 11).
4. *Technological.* This is caused by the use of new techniques and technologies in production, i.e. where a machine replaces a man or where automation replaces mechanization.
5. *Casual.* This type of unemployment encompasses the part-time workers, and those who cannot be certain of their jobs.
6. *Frictional.* This occurs when people leave one job to look for another.
7. *Disguised.* This covers those who are being paid and are not working.
8. *Regional.* This reflects the economic climate of a particular region.
9. *Residual.* This is a catch-all term to describe all other forms of unemployment.

Self-help and community work

Self-help and community projects can help people, with training and advice, and sometimes with small loans, to learn how to make small articles for tourists, such as handicrafts, and to sell in local markets.

The islands of the Caribbean are made up of hundreds of communities, large and small. People who have many and varied common interests are grouped together, usually in government-provided community centres, in schools or in churches, to learn the skill of their chosen craft. The government, through community development departments, provides tutors who are specially trained. The skills taught include shoe-making, leatherwork, dress-making, weaving, woodwork, welding, typing, toy-making and cake-making. These things, though on a small scale, can all aid the economic growth and development of the country by making its citizens more skilled and adaptable.

Community projects also aim to bring people together and to help one another more – to cultivate the 'community spirit'. They help to make the community a better, healthier, safer and more pleasant place in which to live. They help the education of the individual into a better citizen. This community spirit contributes to production and allows the different races and religions of the Caribbean to get along well together as friends and neighbours.

Migration and the labour force

Migration is the permanent movement of people from one area to another or from one country to another. When he leaves one country, the person concerned is an *emigrant;* when he arrives at the other country, he is an *immigrant.* Migration is one of the factors affecting population growth or decline within the area concerned. It is a means of preserving the equilibrium (or balance) between the birth rate and the number of inhabitants that a country can support.

People undertake migration to secure and obtain new homes, more living space, to escape political and economic pressures and to find better jobs and a higher standard of living. Within a country, migration tends to take place from the country to the towns and from depressed areas to thriving industrial areas and the capital.

Migration is bound to have an effect on the labour force in both areas. If the supply of labour is not in equilibrium, it will be impossible for a country to achieve maximum economic growth. If a country has too few workers, this will act as a brake on development and industrial production. If, on the other hand, a country has more inhabitants than it can support, output per head will be low and the standard of living will either be below subsistence level, or the government will have to spend money on public relief payments or food imports instead of releasing it for industrial development. This is a big problem for many 'third-world' countries.

Migration can also have an effect on the labour force because of discrimination. The migrant may find it difficult to get work in his or her new country because of:

1. Sex or race discrimination.
2. Class discrimination and class barriers.
3. Educational qualifications which are not recognized in the new country.
4. Language difficulties.
5. Exploitation of his or her ignorance of the new country.

He or she may have to take low-paid or dirty work, at least to start, and be prepared to live in very bad conditions.

Migration has always been very important to the Caribbean. After the abolition of slavery, many Indian and Chinese workers came in to work on the plantations. In the twentieth century, thousands of West Indians have migrated to Britain and North America. After a while, migration affects the labour force so much that the governments of these countries have to step in. The Canadian, United States and British governments are making it harder for West Indians to migrate to their countries. It is even very difficult to migrate from one Caribbean country to another.

The importance of entrepreneurial skills

Entrepreneur is a French word which means master-builder or contractor. As we saw above, the entrepreneur brings together and organizes the three factors of production, natural resources, labour and capital, and produces useful goods or services at a profit – just as the building contractor brings together on the chosen site the many types of material and skilled labour required to produce a useful building.

The role of the entrepreneur is very important. The modern world is becoming ever more complex. Without his vision and organizing skill, many of the facilities on which we rely in a mixed economy just would not exist. Without his ability to put money to good use, by creating profitable investment opportunities (see Chapter 5), a lot of people with money over and above their immediate needs would not be able to invest it in industries and businesses creating new jobs and new wealth for their country.

The role of capital in production

We have already seen that anyone setting up in business needs *capital.* It is time to define capital more carefully. Unfortunately the word is used in different senses by different groups of people.

1. To the *private citizen,* capital is his savings plus his material possessions – everything that he owns.
2. To the *economist,* capital is the value of goods, such as plant and machinery, whose purpose is to produce consumption goods in the future.
3. To the *accountant,* the capital of a business consists of its assets less its current liabilities, represented by share capital plus accumulated profits (the owner's equity of a sole trader).
4. Finally, when we talk of *capital equipment,* we mean buildings and machinery that have been bought for use over many years.

Some industries are on a larger scale than others. It is obvious that a motor car manufacturer will need much more elaborate and expensive equipment than a baker or producer of meat patties. The car manufacturer will therefore need a much larger capital. Only a large and wealthy country is therefore likely to be able to raise the hundreds of millions of dollars required.

RESEARCH ACTIVITY

Find out, and mark on a map, the natural resources of your country.

Find out what your government is doing to exploit and develop its natural resources.

Find out what industries are linked to the natural resources.

Write a report on this.

To help you:
Look in the telephone directory, under words like Development, Economic Development, Tourism. See if you can find the telephone number and address of any government ministry or other organization concerned with economic development (or some similar title) and ask them for leaflets and information.

The public library may also have information about this and will help you.

SURVEY

Conduct a survey among your family, friends and neighbours at home; ask them to tell you about anyone they know who has emigrated. Where did they go? Why? Make a list of the places people have emigrated to, with the numbers beside each country. Make a second list of the reasons why they went, with numbers beside each reason.

SELF-REVISION QUESTIONS

1. Define production. How may it be sub-divided?
2. Name the four factors of production and give two examples of each.
3. Name the factors that contribute to the supply of labour. Which do you consider the most important in your own country?
4. What do you understand by mobility of labour? How does it differ from migration?
5. Describe a typical self-help or community project.
6. What part do you believe self-help and community projects play in improving the life of the community?
7. For what reasons do people leave the country and migrate to the towns?
8. What would be the advantages and disadvantages to your country if there was complete freedom of migration?
9. What is an entrepreneur?
10. Say, with reasons, which of the following statements best describes the role of the entrepreneur:
    (a) A useless parasite.
    (b) A middleman who performs a useful but minor service.
    (c) An essential part of modern commerce and industry.
11. State the meaning of capital to:
    (a) the economist;
    (b) the accountant.

6

The organization of the factors of production

Levels of production

In the past, when transport was difficult and most people lived in small villages, most production of food was in the hands of small farmers, called peasants or smallholders, each with a small plot of land on which they grew only the crops which they needed to feed themselves and their families. This is called *subsistence farming.* Usually it is not very efficient; the farmer and his wife and children have to work long hours in the fields growing their crops and looking after their animals. Even so they can only produce a small surplus to trade for essential goods like salt, knives and cloth. If bad weather, a drought or hurricane strikes, they will probably go hungry. Such people have very little need for money. This type of production is tending to die out, but is still found in remote country areas and in large parts of Africa and Asia.

The next stage to develop was the *domestic economy.* The farmer grows the type of crops, or keeps the type of livestock, which do best on his soil. He does not try to grow all the food he needs. He will sell all or most of his production in the local markets or to local merchants, and buy what he needs with the money he receives. Obviously a lot more commercial activity will take place in a situation like this. A community of this type is said to be *self-sufficient.* There are many parts of the world where local areas are largely (if not entirely) self-sufficient, at least in food production, though even here a few luxury items will be imported from outside, like tea, coffee and fruit. A development of the self-sufficient domestic economy is the self-sufficient national economy. Here a country decides as a matter of policy that it will grow all the food it needs and not rely on imports except in emergency. The USA tries to grow all its own food.

The third stage is the *cash-crop economy.* Here a country develops a pattern of agriculture where a lot of crops or animals are exported for cash. Sometimes the country will not then be able to grow enough food for its inhabitants, but will rely on its foreign earnings to buy what it needs. This system often develops where a country has a special advantage in its climate or soil, which enables it to grow a crop in world demand which cannot be grown elsewhere. The West Indies pioneered this type of agriculture in the seventeenth and eighteenth centuries with large plantations of sugar cane. At that time only the West Indies and the Southern states of the USA could grow the sugar the world needed. Other well-known examples of cash crops are coffee (especially from Brazil), cocoa (from Ghana) and rubber (from Malaysia).

Cottage industries

A cottage industry (also called *the putting-out system* or *domestic system)* is one which takes place in the worker's own home instead of him or her going out to work in a factory or an office. Traditionally work was distributed to men or women who operated small machines (like weaving frames) in their own homes and were paid piece rates, i.e. so much for each piece or article produced. When more elaborate machinery was invented, which had to be in a factory, the system lost much of its popularity, but it has never completely died out. Today the work is often done by women to supplement the family income.

Pottery is specially made under this system in Trinidad today. Things like pepper sauce, handicrafts and small items of furniture are still produced in this way. Fruit is pickled and bottled, and small garment manufacturers find this system very useful; they send out cloth to be cut out and sewn up into clothes.

The advantages of the cottage industry system are:

1. It minimizes the investment needed by the entrepreneur.
2. The worker can work at home at her own pace, and often look after the family at the same time.
3. It gives the entrepreneur, who puts out the work, more flexibility, as he needs only employ out-workers when there is work to be done; he does not have to pay them wages in slack periods.
4. The worker can often be helped by members of the family.

The disadvantages are:

1. The worker usually has to put in long hours to earn a living.
2. She may get no work (and therefore no money) in slack periods.
3. She can only use simple, cheap machines (like sewing machines) and may not be able to compete with goods produced in a well-equipped factory.

Linkage industries

A linkage industry is one that is linked up with, or dependent on, another industry. For instance, those who produce fertilizers or farm machinery are obviously dependent on agriculture: the industries are *linked.* Other linkage industries which are important in the Caribbean are:

1. The rum industry, the bagasse industry (which uses the wastes from sugar cane to make ceiling boards) and the candy industry are linked up with the sugar industry.
2. The plastics and petro-chemical industries are linked up with the oil industry, because they both use oil as their raw material. All those who make things of plastics, from plastic drinking cups to records, electrical equipment and water pipes, are also dependent on the oil industry.
3. The road-building industry is linked up with the asphalt industry (produced from the Pitch Lake in Trinidad or as a by-product of oil refining).
4. Bauxite is linked to the making of aluminium. The waste from both bauxite and aluminium goes to road building and land filling.

Linkage industries are often sited near the industry on which they are dependent, but modern transport makes this less important, particularly if the materials are light and easy to move about.

Location of industry

There are several factors which may influence industry in choosing the best site for its operations:

1. Closeness to source of supply of raw materials (or to the port through which they are imported).
2. Closeness to markets for the products produced – this is one reason why so many small factories are found on the outskirts of large towns.
3. Closeness to supply of fuel or power – this is less important than it used to be because electricity is fairly cheap to transport.
4. Availability of land of the right type and size at the right price – industries are seldom set up in city centres or in the middle of a swamp.
5. Availability of labour.
6. Good access and transport facilities – e.g. sawmills on rivers.

7. Government controls – these are becoming increasingly important as a factor influencing location of industry, and months of negotiation may take place before the site for a large factory or refinery is decided.
8. Climatic conditions are important in deciding where to grow agricultural products. For example, the slopes of the Blue Mountain in Jamaica are very suitable for the high-quality coffee for which the island is famous; in Grenada, nutmegs are grown at relatively high altitudes with the right combination of high rainfall (over 200cm p.a.) and moderate temperature (below 24°C).
9. Linkage industries will naturally grow up near the industries on which they depend – suppliers of drilling equipment will tend to be located near oil or gas fields.

Despite all these factors, growth of a particular industry may depend on accident or tradition. There is no logical reason, for instance, why Switzerland should have become a centre of the watch and clock industry.

Advantages and disadvantages of scale

An industry operating on a large scale tends to have the following advantages over competitors operating on a smaller scale:

1. It can afford to install more expensive and efficient machinery.
2. It will employ more workers, so more of them can be specialists (see advantages of division of labour in Chapter 1).
3. It will place larger orders for its supplies and get better prices or bigger discounts from its suppliers.
4. It can afford to pay for more research and development work, leading to better products in the future.
5. It can employ more salespeople and run bigger advertising campaigns, thus maximizing its sales.
6. It can negotiate better terms for its loans from the banks, and get loans more easily, because it can offer better collateral (security).
7. It can offer better welfare and training to its employees, and a better career structure for internal promotions.
8. Its greater financial resources will make it easier to survive when business is bad.

On the other hand, there are also disadvantages:

1. The operations can grow too big for the management to control properly, which can lead to slackness, waste, inter-departmental squabbles, pilfering and low morale.

2. Because of its massive investment in machinery and other specialized equipment, it can lose the flexibility necessary to respond quickly to changes in demand.
3. Business may be lost because those who take the decisions are out of touch with the customers.
4. There is a danger of unnecessary paperwork and administrative staff being taken on board, thus raising costs.
5. If it has a large share of the market for its products, it may be subjected to government intervention in the form of price controls or other restrictions.

The best size for a business will largely depend on the amount of capital and equipment needed for efficient operation. Thus motor car manufacturers, oil companies and high technology industries like the chemical and electronics industries have to be large; but there are few advantages of scale for firms of solicitors or accountants. However, in many trades, large and small firms operate side by side. The small trader may overcome his handicaps by extra efficiency, ingenuity and hard work.

Role and function of the small firm

It was noted above that, although businesses are growing in size and complexity, the large firm tends to suffer from certain disadvantages. Thus the small firm can still compete. It can also stay open longer hours and offer personal service to its customers. Many small businesses are run by the owner and his family, operating from their own home; they can therefore cut costs and undertake things like minor repairs which the larger business, with expensive shop premises and a high wages bill, would not find economic.

The function of the small firm in the economy is very important.

1. In many small towns and villages, and in many small islands, the small business is the only business that is possible.
2. Big trees can only grow from small seedlings. Nearly all new businesses start on a small scale, even though they may grow big later. A man starting out in business will only have a small capital, and therefore his business must be on a small scale. Without small businesses, many new ideas would never be tried out.
3. Small firms provide competition to the big firms and stop them from becoming inefficient and putting up their prices too much; the big store will soon lose customers if the same goods can be bought for less in the small shop round the corner.

4. Many people set up in business in a small way as a means of supplementing their regular income, whether as farmers, fishermen or factory workers. This can be particularly important where their work is *seasonal,* i.e. only available for part of the year.
5. Some businesses, such as a taxi service, are difficult to control if run on a large scale, but if the driver runs his own taxi as a small business, he will do this more efficiently, because his livelihood depends on it.

Many governments recognize these factors and encourage small businesses by charging them less tax, or exempting them from certain taxes altogether. In some cases loans are available to small-business managers at special rates.

Capital- and labour-intensive industries

Some industries are more *capital-intensive* than others. A capital-intensive industry requires a large investment in capital equipment and comparatively few workers to run it; a good example is an oil refinery. A *labour-intensive* industry, on the other hand, requires a large number of workers but not nearly so much capital investment. Most service industries are labour-intensive; examples are the post office, the tourist industry and the transport industry.

The tendency is for more and more equipment to be installed to do work faster and better than it can be done by hand. This means more and more expense, so that more capital is required. The ways this capital is raised are discussed in Chapter 9, but if people are to be encouraged to invest their spare money (rather than spend it), then the government must do two things:

1. It must make the country as prosperous as possible and allow industry to make reasonable profits without excessive taxation, so that the investor gets a good return on his or her money.
2. It must keep inflation in check so that the value of his investment not whittled away – if someone invests $100 at 10% interest but inflation is running at 20% per annum, at the end of the year he or she will have $110 in paper money but this will be worth $91.67 in comparative buying power.

The only alternative, if the country is not to fall behind in the industrial race, is for the government itself to provide the capital for investment in industry.

Automation and mechanization

Mechanization means replacing human or animal muscle-power by machine, which can usually do the job more quickly and efficiently. Thus when a tailor buys a sewing machine, instead of sewing up garments by hand, he is mechanizing his work. The machine is much more expensive than a simple needle and thread, but as it enables him to do his work much faster, it soon pays for itself if the volume of work is high enough. The same principle operates when a farmer replaces his donkey and cart with a truck or tractor. More and more mechanization has been taking place over the last 200 years, but the availability of electricity and small, cheap petrol and diesel engines has greatly speeded up the process.

Automation is mechanization taken a stage further. When an operation is merely mechanized, it still has to be carried out by a worker (or series of workers), although there are power tools and machines to help. When a process is automated, a whole series of operations is carried out automatically without human intervention; all that the operator has to do is to start the process off, see that all is well and press the 'Stop' button if something goes wrong. Automation in industry usually involves a massive investment of millions of dollars, so only the industrial giants can afford it. But there are some homes too which boast a simple version of automation, the automatic washing machine, which can be loaded with clothes and will then soak, wash, rinse and spin-dry them, and finally turn itself off, without further attention.

With advances in technology, especially with computers becoming daily cheaper and more sophisticated, automation is spreading to many more types of process control. Many systems are even programmed to reject sub-standard output or adjust their setting if items start being produced which are outside strictly controlled limits of size, shape or weight.

The advantages of automation are:

1. Fewer workers are needed, thus reducing labour costs.
2. Output can usually be speeded up.
3. It reduces the chance of human error, and results in more uniform output.
4. The computer, which performs automated data-processing, can perform in minutes calculations which would take many weeks by hand, with a high risk of mistake – so the computer can do things which it would not be practical to do otherwise
5. Because of the reduction in time and labour, many goods produced automatically are cheaper.
6. It acts as a spur to technological education and scientific research,

because the profits to be made from successful inventions can be very great.

The disadvantages are:

1. Many of those thrown out of work may find it difficult to get another job, i.e. it tends to increase unemployment.
2. If a mistake is made in setting up an automated process, it can result in a lot of damage and be very expensive to correct.
3. The machines need highly skilled technicians to run and repair them; they are often in short supply.
4. Because automated equipment is so expensive, the risk of loss in case of failure is very great. It also requires a large capital, which may be difficult to raise.
5. It may lead to the decline of small and medium-sized firms and a consequent decline in competition.

PLANNING TASKS

Imagine you are going to set up a cottage industry. Find out what cottage industries there are in your country. Will you choose one of those? Or some idea of your own? Plan how you will set it up. Where will you get the money to obtain the materials? What materials will you need? How will you sell your products? Write about what you will do.

Imagine you are going to open a hotel. Make a list of the factors which will be important in choosing a location for your hotel. Look at property for sale in your newspaper and see if there is a site or a building for sale in any suitable location. Write a report on what is available, and the advantages and disadvantages of the location of each site.

RESEARCH TASKS

Choose a small business in your neighbourhood. Find out how it is useful to people. Write a short report for a newspaper about this firm.

Find out, using information at your library, or looking up 'Small Businesses' or 'Finance and development' in the telephone directory, what the government does to help small businesses. Write a short column of advice about this for a newspaper.

SELF-REVISION QUESTIONS

1. What do you understand by subsistence farming? Are there any parts of the Caribbean where this is still practised?
2. Discuss the relative advantages of growing cash crops for export and of self-sufficiency in agricultural products. Illustrate your answer with local examples if possible.
3. State whether you think the cottage industry system is a good or bad system:
   (a) for the workers;
   (b) for the employer.
4. Give three examples of linkage industries. Describe what you think might happen to the other industry if one of the linked industries was forced to close down.
5. List the factors influencing the location of industry.
6. Take one important industry established in your country and discuss which factor was most important in determining its location.
7. List the advantages to be gained from large-scale production.
8. What is the difference between a capital-intensive industry and a labour-intensive industry? Give an example of each. Which type is more typical of the Caribbean?
9. How can investment in industry be encouraged?
10. Explain the difference between automation and mechanization.
11. What are the advantages and disadvantages of automation:
    (a) to the worker?
    (b) to the industrialist?
    (c) to the customer?

7

Marketing

Markets and marketing

A market exists under any conditions when a number of buyers and sellers are brought together. A market can be any of the following:

1. A building or place where people meet to buy and sell their products. There are several such markets in the Caribbean. In every city and town one will find a place set aside for a market and operated by the local council. In populous areas there can be more than one market, some of them specialized markets, like markets for the sale of fish and seafood only. Most stallholders in markets are engaged in selling foodstuffs direct to the consumers.
2. A hall or building set up for the buying and selling of commodities in large quantities between businessmen, often importers on the one side and merchants or manufacturers on the other. Examples are the tea and metal exchanges in London. Although this type of market is only found in a very few large cities such as London or New York, it plays a very important part in international trade.
3. A stock exchange is a specialized type of market for buying and selling stocks and shares.
4. Trading such as described in paragraph (2) above can take place without the buyers and sellers ever coming face to face. The buying and selling of foreign currencies, for example, takes place between bankers and brokers in many parts of the world, who communicate with each other by telephone or by new electronic means.
5. Finally, a large group of people likely to buy a given product or service are described by its providers as the 'market' for that product or service. Conversely, when something is not likely to sell well, people will say there is 'no market' for it.

It is this last use of the word market which gave rise to the term *marketing,* which, as mentioned earlier, can be defined as *the discovery and satisfaction of consumers' needs at a profit.* It covers very much more than selling, though selling is a very important part of marketing.

For the very small trader, keeping in touch with market requirements may be very simple. Someone selling items at a street-corner will soon discover which of the things on sale is in demand, how other street traders nearby are doing, and how high prices can go before the customers stop buying. In large firms, perhaps operating on an international scale, the decisions may be taken by top managers who never meet their customers face to face, and it is by them that modern marketing techniques have been developed to enable them to keep in touch with their markets and keep their sales and profit figures at a maximum.

Market research

Market research covers the collection and interpretation of facts that are relevant to any part of the activity of marketing. It can be divided into four main phases:

1. *Fundamental market research.* What sort of new products should the company be making? Should the company diversify into new fields, or should it concentrate on improving its existing line of business?
2. *Product development.* Once the company has decided what to produce, the results must be tested by asking groups of customers their opinion of it, before risking millions of dollars on full-scale production. This covers such things as the best size, price, colour, type of packaging.
3. *Distribution.* What are the best outlets for the product? Should it be sold direct to retailers or only to wholesalers? Should the company have its own sales force, or use agents?
4. *Advertising* or *media research.* This covers the best means of publicizing the product at the least cost. Is it best to launch the product with one big bang or spread the publicity over a longer period?

Market research consists mostly of asking people questions, although this will be backed up by gathering facts from reference books, newspapers, rival producers' catalogues, etc. (called *desk research*). A list of questions, called a *questionnaire,* is drawn up. This is skilled work; it is essential that the questions are not misunderstood, lead to a clear answer that can be accurately recorded, and are a true test of people's reactions without putting ideas into their head. The two main means of conducting surveys are:

1. *By post.* This is simple and cheap; the main disadvantage is that a lot of people do not bother to complete and return their questionnaire.
2. *By personal interview.* Interviewers are sent out to knock on doors or stop people in the street, ask them the questions on the form and record their answers. This can be expensive.

Surveys can be of various types, depending on the purpose for which they are required. The four main types are:

1. *Opinion surveys* – for example, 'Which brand of toothpaste do you think is the best?'
2. *Factual surveys* – 'Which brand of toothpaste did you use this morning?'
3. *Attitude surveys* – used to test out two or three alternatives to see which is most popular.
4. *Future intention surveys* – for example, 'Do you intend to buy a new car within the next year, and if so, what model?'

It is impossible to ask every possible consumer his or her views. Instead, *a sample* (selection) is chosen which is *representative* of the population as a whole – for instance, it must include poor people as well as rich, country as well as town dwellers, old as well as young and middle-aged. The two most popular means of choosing the sample are:

1. *Quota sampling.* Each interviewer is told to go to a specific area and select a given number (quota) of interviewees of a specific type.
2. *Random sampling.* Random does not mean haphazard – in fact random sampling can be more precise than quota sampling. People are chosen at random from a list, such as the voters' register, by using a table of random numbers, and these specific people are interviewed. The idea is to eliminate any form of bias, prejudice or imbalance which might otherwise creep in. Special rules have to be laid down to cope with those who have died, left the district or refuse to answer.

The size of the sample is decided by statisticians. A larger sample is more expensive to interview than a small one, but usually gives more accurate results.

Advertising

This is the art of putting the good points of a product or service or idea to the public. If advertising is to succeed, people must not only notice the message, but remember it and act on it too. The claims made must be credible, clear, striking and carried in the right advertising medium; for example, specialized medical equipment would be advertised in specialized medical journals, while medicines to be sold over the pharmacy counter might be advertised in the daily newspapers.

Every year millions of dollars are spent on advertising in the Caribbean alone. Sometimes the advertising costs more than the raw materials! Yet manufacturers consider it worthwhile. It is their main means of bringing new products to the attention of the public, and of reminding them about established ones.

Advertising can be loosely grouped into four main types: informative, persuasive, collective/generic, and competitive.

1. *Informative.* This aims at 'informing and educating' the consumer about a particular product or service.
2. *Persuasive.* This makes an attempt to persuade or convince the consumer to buy a particular product or service.
3. *Collective/Generic.* This type of advertising tells the consumer to buy a particular product or service in general, not necessarily any particular brand (e.g. advertising rum, not a specific brand of rum).
4. *Competitive.* This is the type in which the producer puts forward the good points about his product or service and compares it with a competing product or service, the chief aim being to influence the consumer not to buy similar goods from a different manufacturer.

Small businesses may handle their own advertising, whereas large organizations employ specialist advertising agencies to assist them. These will suggest the most effective line of attack, select and book the space or time required, write the copy, arrange for the photographs or pictures to be prepared and see to the printing if necessary.

Some professions like doctors, dentists and lawyers are not allowed to advertise. Advertising should paint a true picture of the product; it should be fair and honest. It is for this reason that operators of television stations, radio stations, newspapers and magazines may refuse to accept an advertisement which they think makes false claims. The advertising of some items, such as drugs, is also controlled by law. The advantages of advertising are:

1. It informs the public about the goods and services that are available. (This is particularly important if they are new.)
2. It assists competition by keeping the consumer informed of the alternative products on the market.
3. It increases sales, thus keeping costs down through economies of scale.

4. Because the makers of a well-advertised product expect the public to buy it time after time, it encourages production of goods of a consistently high standard.
5. It helps manufacturers and shopkeepers alike to increase their sales, thus increasing prosperity and employment.
6. Without the revenue from advertising, many TV and radio stations could not exist, and newspapers would be more expensive.

However, advertising is also strongly criticized from time to time. The main grounds for complaint are:

1. It often deceives the public through exaggerated and untrue claims.
2. It is a waste of resources which could be put to better use.
3. The high cost of advertising is paid for by the consumer in the form of higher prices.
4. It encourages people, particularly those with poor education, to buy things they do not need and/or cannot afford.

The possible advertising media are very numerous. The most popular are:

- Radio and television.
- Newspapers and magazines.
- Posters and handbills.
- Shop window displays.
- Circulars and catalogues.
- Printed messages on calendars, paper bags, etc.
- Messages painted on buses, trucks and vans.

Sales promotion

In one sense, anything that promotes (encourages) sales may be considered as 'sales promotion' – virtually everything discussed in this chapter. However, among marketing experts the phrase has come to have a more restricted meaning – special schemes, often running for only a limited period, encouraging retailers to stock and consumers to buy the product. Some well-known tactics are: 'five cents off' (temporary price reductions); 'free gifts' such as artificial flowers or plastic teaspoons given away with detergent packets; coupon schemes, where items are sent free or at a low price in return for a certain number of packet tops; trading stamps; coupons in cigarette packets; and simple competitions, with the entry form printed on the packet. Many other schemes are devised; the keys to success are originality and ingenuity.

Such promotions are particularly effective in getting consumers to try a new product. However, the effect is only temporary unless the product itself is good and it is backed by strong advertising.

Public relations

Public relations (PR) is another specialized aspect of the marketing effort. Its aim is a long-term one – to make the public and the government well disposed towards the company and its products. It takes several forms: encouraging newspapers to publish articles about the company and its products; having people prepared to answer questions about the company from the press and public; preparing leaflets on the use of products for schoolteachers, housewives, etc. Only the largest companies can afford specialist PR staff, but even the smallest business should make sure that all its staff, from the managing director to shop assistants, give a good impression to the public.

Packaging and branding

Originally a 'brand' was a hot iron used to burn a mark in the hides of cattle, to show to whom they belonged. Each farmer or rancher had his own, easily recognizable brand mark. The word was soon used for the special designs or names which manufacturers gave to their products. It started with such things as polish, rum and patent medicines, which from the earliest days were packed or bottled at the factory. Branding has become even more important today as more and more goods are pre-packed, and fewer and fewer sold loose, or packed and weighed over the grocer's counter.

Packaging (which includes glass and plastic bottles and jars as well as cardboard packets) was at first used simply to protect the item in transit, but manufacturers soon realized the value of the packaging for identifying and advertising the product. Today, almost as much care is taken over designing the packaging of anything from a scent bottle to a paperback novel, as over its advertising on radio, press or television. With the growth in self-service and supermarkets, a product that does not call attention to itself on the shelf just does not get bought.

The sales force

Despite all the means of persuasion and communication so far discussed, nothing is quite so persuasive as a good salesperson. This is why manufacturers are prepared to spend large sums of money on paying and equipping teams of salespeople to call on shopkeepers, industrial customers and government purchasing departments. A large company will have its own sales force, administered by a sales manager. A very large company may have several different sales forces, each with its own manager, covering different areas of the world or different types of product. Smaller companies may use agents or freelance salespeople (selling the goods of more than one manufacturer).

Careful note is taken of the sales coming in from each salesperson's 'territory' or area. Periodic sales conferences are held, when salespeople are briefed on new products and discuss tactics such as which lines are to be pursued with the greatest vigour. Salespeople may be paid a salary, a *commission* (a percentage of the sales they make), or a combination of both; in the last case, the salesperson's commission may also be known as a *bonus.* Sometimes the bonus is only paid after a pre-determined target or budgeted level of sales has been reached.

Good salespeople will possess the following characteristics:

1. A thorough knowledge of their products.
2. A good understanding of human nature and the customer's point of view. This will enable them to stress those benefits of the product most likely to appeal to the customer.
3. Energy and drive, combined with courtesy and patience.
4. An outgoing, friendly nature. This puts the customer at ease and gives him instinctive confidence in the salesperson and the product.
5. The ability to plan their attack and their day so that they do not waste time on fruitless visits.
6. The ability to see and understand how their competitors work.

Many salespeople do more than simply sell. They may provide (or arrange) after-sales service (particularly with complicated products or machinery), or be responsible for *merchandizing,* that is, persuading the customer to give a good display of the product, and sometimes actually putting it on the shelf for him, as well as supplying showcards, window stickers and other *point-of-sale display* items.

Trade associations and chambers of commerce

A *chamber of commerce* is an organization of the principal business concerns of a town or area. They originated in Jersey, Channel Islands, in 1768. In the Caribbean there are many chambers of commerce in the main towns.

The principal objects of a chamber of commerce are:

1. To promote home and foreign trade in general, and especially the trade of the district in which the chamber is situated.
2. To discuss legislation affecting trade and to support or oppose it where necessary.
3. To watch carefully the administration of Acts of Parliament affecting trade, and to press the police or government departments to enforce them where necessary.
4. To co-operate with other chambers of commerce.
5. To review legislation of foreign countries likely to affect trade, and to press the government to make protests where necessary.
6. To review the impact of customs and excise duties, and foreign exchange regulations.
7. To sign consular invoices and certificates of origin. (These documents are sometimes required in international trade.)
8. To give members information and advice on:
   (a) Customs tariffs and exchange control regulations of other countries.
   (b) Appointment of agents abroad.
   (c) Recovery of debts at home and abroad.
   (d) The law of trade marks and patents.
   (e) Foreign travel regulations (visa and vaccination requirements etc.).
   (f) Export regulations and documentation.
9. To settle disputes between members (if they so agree).

A *trade association* is rather like a chamber of commerce, except that it consists of a grouping of traders in the same line of business, usually on a national basis. Typical examples are the Taxi Drivers' Association, the Citrus Growers' Association and the Association of Travel Agents in Trinidad. Their objects vary slightly from trade to trade, but might be:

1. To exchange information.
2. To agree standard terms and conditions of supply, carriage, etc.
3. To establish a common body for conducting wage negotiations with the trade unions.
4. To protect the interests of members when threatened by government action, tax increases, etc.
5. To conduct joint research and run a technical information service.
6. To collect statistics and distribute them to members.
7. To introduce agreed standard gradings and product descriptions.
8. To give credit information to members.
9. To advise members on foreign trade facilities and regulations.

10. To undertake joint publicity campaigns, at home or abroad, when considered necessary.

In some cases, governments may be prepared to negotiate with, or give information to, a recognized trade association, but not with or to individual firms. This is to avoid all suspicion of giving an unfair advantage to one firm compared to another.

Credit sales and hire purchase

Many people cannot afford to pay in one lump sum the full purchase price of consumer durables such as cars, refrigerators or television sets. However, they are able to pay for them if allowed to do so in instalments over one or two years. Various 'Buy now and pay later' schemes have been devised to make this possible.

1. *Hire purchase.* The customer receives the goods on a down payment, which is usually between one-quarter and one-third of the full price. He agrees to pay the balance, including interest and service charges, by weekly, fortnightly or monthly payments. The goods remain the property of the seller until all the instalments are paid off, and the customer's instalments are regarded legally as fees for hiring the goods – hence the name 'hire purchase'. If the customer fails to keep up the payments, the seller can, under certain conditions, reclaim the goods.

   In the past, poor and uneducated people have often been exploited under this system, so strict government regulations have been introduced in most countries along the following lines:
   (a) In every transaction, the cash price, the down payment and the monthly instalments, as well as the total to be paid under HP must be specified in writing.
   (b) The rights and duties of both parties must be specified in a written agreement which both parties must sign.
   (c) The customer may terminate the agreement by returning the goods, provided that they are in good condition and at least half the instalments have been paid.
   (d) Sometimes the law requires a minimum down payment.
2. *Instalment selling.* This is the same as hire purchase, with the important exception that the goods become the property of the customer as soon as he has made his down payment. If the customer fails to pay his instalments, the seller must sue him in the courts for the money due. He cannot repossess the goods unless the court has ordered the customer to pay up and he still has not done so.

3. *Credit selling.* This is what is called 'trust' in the Caribbean. There is no down payment, no interest charge; the customer takes the goods and pays for them later. This is widely used by small shopkeepers in country areas for items such as groceries bought by regular customers. However, large department stores may run a variation of this scheme; they may open credit accounts for favoured customers, who, instead of paying cash, charge purchases to their account and are sent a monthly statement, which is, in effect, a request for payment.
4. *Lay-away plan.* The customer puts down a deposit. The goods are put aside for him and handed over when he has completed his instalments. This is not strictly a credit transaction, but the customer is protected against price fluctuations.
5. *Mortgages.* These are mainly used for house purchase. The purchaser receives a loan from a bank or insurance company, giving the lender the title deeds of the house as security. The loan is paid off in equal instalments, which are a mixture of interest payments and repayment of capital. If the borrower fails to keep up his instalments, the lender is entitled to sell the house; he will take what is necessary to pay off the loan and hand over the balance to the unfortunate borrower. Most people taking out a mortgage also take out a *mortgage protection* insurance policy, which guarantees that the loan will be paid off should they die.

A shopkeeper selling goods on HP or instalments will not receive full payment for some while, yet may need the cash in order to buy new stock. To get round this difficulty, he may sell the debt to a commercial bank or finance company (a special type of bank), although he may continue to receive the instalments on behalf of the bank. Under HP, the goods then legally belong to the bank or finance company.

The advantages of credit selling are:

1. Consumers can have the advantage of the use of goods at an earlier stage than if they had to save up the whole purchase price.
2. It stimulates trade. Retailers and manufacturers will have a greater turnover. More employment is created.
3. In times of inflation, the consumer may obtain the goods at a cheaper price, even after allowing for interest payments.

The disadvantages are:

1. Consumers may be tempted to buy goods which they cannot really afford.

2. The consumer may not be able to keep up his instalments. In this case the goods may be repossessed, but the consumer will not get back the money already paid.
3. The interest charged is often very high. The total cost to the consumer can be much higher than if he paid cash.
4. Choice may be restricted.
5. There will be a lot of bad debts for the supplier or finance company.
6. The administrative costs are higher than for cash sales.
7. The supplier will either need greater capital to finance the credit (as explained above), or have to go to a finance company which may charge a high commission for taking over the debt.
8. Governments often think that the system encourages inflation.

Trade and cash discounts

A *discount is* a reduction in cost which manufacturers and traders frequently allow to their customers. For example, if the normal price of an item is \$10 and a 20% discount is allowed, the price is reduced to \$10 – 2 = \$8.

Such reductions are only made when it is essential – either because the supplier thinks it will result in a larger order, or because no order at all will result unless a discount is allowed. Their purpose is to introduce greater flexibility into the pricing structure. A manufacturer will probably only produce one price list, which he circulates to all his customers, large and small, and perhaps also to members of the public; the price charged to various customers is varied by allowing them different rates of discount. Naturally, these discounts must be taken into account when calculating selling prices.

There are three principal types:

1. *Trade discount.* This is a discount which manufacturers or wholesalers allow to their customers 'within the trade' – that is, retailers. The goods are invoiced at what is to be their full selling price to the ultimate consumers, but the retailer is permitted to deduct the 'trade discount', which amounts to his gross profit margin. The system enables the seller to indicate clearly at what price he expects the goods to be re-sold; it also permits him to give different retailers different rates of discount while enabling the seller to circulate one price list to all, including the public. Trade discount is always deductible, no matter when the account is paid.
2. *Quantity discount.* Quantity discount is an additional discount which is deductible from the invoiced price and is sometimes allowed where large orders are involved. Quite often, several rates of

quantity discount are quoted – the greater the amount being ordered, the greater the quantity discount allowed.

3. *Cash discount.* This is the best-known form of discount and its purpose is solely to encourage customers to pay their accounts quickly. If the amount is paid before a specified date, then the customer is entitled to deduct a stated percentage from the invoiced price. It is important to note that cash discount is deductible on the amount due *after* trade and quantity discounts have been deducted. For example, if 100 items at $2 were ordered subject to a trade discount of 20% and a cash discount of 5% if paid within 30 days, the calculation of the amount due would be:

	$
Invoice price: 100 @ $2	200
Less trade discount at 20%	40
	$160
5% cash discount for payment within 30 days	8
Net amount payable	$152

(Note that if the amount is not paid within 30 days, then the cash discount would not be allowed and the sum of $160 would have to be paid.)

In certain circumstances a customer who has been sent slightly damaged or imperfect goods may receive a *rebate*. Normally the supplier would have to take the goods back, but the customer may be prepared to accept them if the amount he has to pay is reduced.

Consumer protection

In the old days there was a legal phrase *Caveat emptor* – 'Let the buyer beware'. This meant that it was up to the buyer to ensure that the goods were what they were supposed to be, and to test that they were in working order; if he failed to check, he had no one to blame but himself if he got a bad buy. He was protected in theory against fraudulent practices such as short weight from rigged scales, but there was no systematic check on the accuracy of traders' weights and measures.

It was realized that this was not satisfactory. It is impossible for most people to check that a complicated piece of machinery is in full working order, or that a sealed package contains what is on the label, before agreeing to buy. A major change was introduced by the British Sale of Goods Act 1893, which protects the consumer as follows:

1. All goods sold must be *of merchantable quality*, that is to say, reasonably fit for the purpose for which they are intended. A watch which does not keep reasonably good time is not of merchantable quality.

Buyers of goods which fail to meet this test are entitled to free repair or money compensation. A lower standard would be applied to second-hand goods. A buyer has no redress over a defect which was pointed out at the time of purchase, or would be obvious on inspection, e.g. a chair with a broken leg.

2. Where goods are sold by sample, the *bulk must correspond with the sample.* If you order cloth from a sample in a pattern-book, you have the right to insist that the cloth when delivered is of the same material, weight, pattern and colour.
3. Where goods are sold by description, *goods must correspond with the description.* If you order a specific model of car, you are not obliged to accept a substitute. This is important protection against the practice known as 'switch selling', where a housewife orders, say, a cheap vacuum cleaner and is then asked to pay for a more expensive model, because the original model is 'out of stock' or 'no longer in production'.

The above was valuable but not enough. Unfortunately many consumers were not aware of their rights. They were also swindled by dishonest traders giving short weight, short change and 'seconds' passed off as perfect merchandise. So most countries have introduced *consumer education campaigns,* run by the government or voluntary consumer organizations, which issue pamphlets or give radio broadcasts explaining consumers' rights, publish comparative test reports on the performance and price of different brands of goods, and press for changes in the law if they think they are necessary.

Most countries have also passed new laws in recent years which supplement the protection given by the Sale of Goods Act:

1. *Weights and measures inspectors* go round checking the accuracy of shopkeepers' scales and measuring sticks, and checking that things like loaves of bread are of the prescribed weight.
2. *Public health inspectors* and *analysts* check that goods are pure and safe to eat, and contain minimum quantities of certain ingredients. For example, they will test samples of milk to check that it does not contain harmful tuberculosis bacilli and has not been watered down.
3. Traders can be prosecuted for false *description* of goods, for instance describing something made with skimmed milk as 'full cream', or a cheap fabric like rayon as 'silk', or something as 'shatterproof' when it isn't.
4. *Bogus price reductions* are prohibited, for instance an article marked as 'Reduced to $14.99', when it has never been sold at any other price.

5. *Bogus guarantees* which try to take away consumers' normal legal rights may be declared invalid.
6. Where *trading stamps* are issued, they must have a specific cash value printed on them, and be redeemable for that sum (not only in exchange of goods).
7. *Misleading advertisements* may be illegal. For instance, it is no longer allowed to advertise a patent medicine as a cancer cure.

However, all these measures will only be partly effective unless consumers themselves are on their guard. They should count their change. They should make sure that they get the oranges they asked for, and not bruised or dried-up ones produced from a box at the back of the stall. If they have cause for complaint, they should complain, to the shopkeeper or trader in the first instance, and, if they get no satisfaction, to the appropriate government department. They will be helping others as well as themselves.

The chain of distribution

Very seldom is it possible or sensible for the manufacturer or producer to sell his products direct to the final consumer. Instead, products will pass through various hands before they reach the end of the chain of distribution, as shown in the diagram (Figure 7.1).

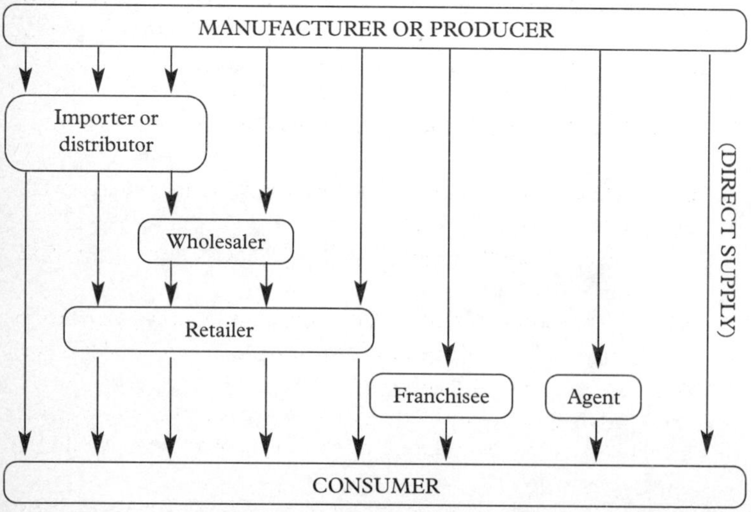

Figure 7.1 Distribution channels

The most important links in the chain are the *wholesaler* and the *retailer*. Retailers own the shops to be found in any town or village; the various types of shop are discussed in the next section. Wholesalers are less often in the public eye; their premises are often inconspicuous and sited in the back streets or on industrial estates where rentals are cheaper. They perform important services as *middlemen,* standing between the manufacturer and the retailer. The advantages of the wholesalers to the manufacturer are:

1. They buy goods in large quantities and store them until bought from them in small quantities by retailers. This is important, because it is much cheaper for a manufacturer to supply one order for 1,000 cartons of a product than ten orders for 100 each.
2. One wholesaler will supply dozens of retailers. This cuts down the number of accounts for the manufacturer to deal with.
3. Most wholesalers have considerable capital resources and can safely be supplied on credit; this would not be possible with many smaller retailers, particularly outside the manufacturer's own country.
4. Wholesalers are experts in ordering goods from far away and know how to deal with import controls, etc., while retailers like a source of supply close at hand.
5. Many wholesalers have their own salespeople who sell the goods they stock to retailers, which manufacturers would find difficult or impossible to call on direct.
6. Wholesalers often have a better idea of the likes and dislikes of consumers in their area than manufacturers could gain for themselves.

The advantages of the wholesaler to the retailer are:

1. He is close at hand – the manufacturer may be hundreds of kilometres away or even overseas.
2. The retailer can obtain the goods he needs much more quickly than from the manufacturer.
3. The retailer can obtain all his requirements, which may come from all parts of the world, through only two or three wholesalers. This makes ordering and accounting easier.
4. The retailer can usually obtain credit from the wholesaler, whereas the manufacturer, to whom he would be unknown, would be unlikely to give it.
5. The retailer can buy in small quantities. He need not tie up large sums of money in slow-moving stock.

6. The retailer may be able to inspect the goods in the wholesaler's warehouse before deciding whether to take them.

It should be noted that it is quite common for a wholesaler to have his own retail shop as well as selling to other retailers. Many wholesalers have branch warehouses; for instance, a Trinidadian wholesaler might have warehouses in Port of Spain, San Fernando and Scarborough (Tobago), perhaps also in Barbados, Guyana, Grenada, etc. Some wholesalers deliver goods free, while others deliver goods for a charge. In the Caribbean they usually do not deliver goods to retailers unless their salespeople book orders from retailers or do road selling.

At each stage in the chain goods increase in price as each trader takes his profit on the transaction. For this reason, it is sometimes said that goods would be cheaper, or retailers could make better profits, if middlemen such as wholesalers were abolished. The truth is that if it were possible to do without wholesalers, businesspeople would have found a way of doing so. Retailers and manufacturers both find that the services outlined above are well worth the extra that they have to pay. Large retailers such as department stores will usually buy direct from manufacturers but they perform the wholesaling functions of storage and breaking bulk within their own warehouses and distribution systems.

In the distribution chain, *importers* can be considered as wholesalers who specialize in goods imported from overseas. *Franchisees* often run petrol service stations, laundromats, fast food counters, etc. They are given technical advice, help with fitting out their premises and advertising signs by the producer of the petrol, etc. that they sell, and in return undertake not to sell competing brands. *Agents* are more often found in the services (such as insurance) and in industrial goods; they seldom own the goods they sell, but take orders for the manufacturer in return for a commission.

Types of retail outlet

As explained in the previous section, the retailer is the last link in the distribution chain before the goods reach the consumer. He sells in even smaller quantities – one jar, one packet, one box of matches – and usually for cash, though he may grant limited credit to regular customers. However, not all retailers are involved in selling goods. They may also offer a service, such as tailoring, cleaning or repairs. Many retailers have comparatively little capital; they will hope to sell most of the goods they stock before they have to pay the wholesaler's bill. Even for large retailers, a quick turnover of stock is important if they are to make a profit.

Retail outlets can be broadly divided into small-scale and large-scale. The main types of *small-scale retail outlet* in the Caribbean are:

1. *Automats* (vending machines). These are strategically sited in bus stations, airports, offices, hotels, etc. The range of goods and services supplied in this way is constantly expanding – photographs, recorded music, hot and cold drinks – but most sell cigarettes or confectionery. The great advantage is that they can be 'open' 24 hours a day; the owner or his agent comes round regularly to check that the machine is working properly, to restock and to collect the money. The main drawbacks are that they may run out of stock, break down or suffer from theft, vandalism or counterfeit or foreign coins being inserted.
2. *Mobile shops.* They sell goods that are in regular demand, serving suburbs, residential districts and country areas where there are few regular shops. Many housewives prefer to buy from them because shopping can be done in front of their own doorsteps. The range of goods they carry is naturally restricted.
3. *Itinerant traders.* Itinerant means 'moving about', but under this heading can be included people who sell produce at their own front door, as well as hawkers, pedlars and market vendors. They usually specialize in one or two products which are easy to carry, such as coconuts or snow-cones. They perform a very valuable service to the community. This is a very flexible form of retailing; they can set up shop very quickly almost anywhere and need very little equipment. The only dangers are that some may be selling stolen goods, and there is no 'come-back' if things like wristwatches do not work.
4. *General stores.* These are the village shops found all over the Caribbean. They sell not only food but virtually all the types of goods that their customers need.
5. *Specialist shops.* These specialize in selling one or two items only, for instance, record shops or bookshops, or a range of connected items, such as hardware or drugs (pharmacies).
6. *Tied shops.* These were mentioned in the previous section. Petrol stations and motor car dealers are good examples. They are so called because the owner is tied more or less to selling one manufacturer's goods, in return for specialist equipment and advertising support. The main disadvantage of this type of outlet is that there is no choice, either for the customer or the proprietor; the customer can take his custom elsewhere, but the owner may suffer if the goods he sells become uncompetitive because of poor quality or high prices.

The main types of *large-scale retail outlet* are:

1. *Manufacturers' own shops.* Some manufacturers prefer to sell their own products and so have set up a chain of retail shops. Clearly, it is only worth their while to do so if the demand for their products is regular and extensive. Customers must also have a large variety of goods from which to choose, and the demand must not be seasonal. Perhaps the best-known example in the Caribbean are the Bata shoe shops.
2. *Multiple shops or chain stores.* Multiple shops are defined as retail businesses having ten or more branches. Some are national, while other chains, such as Woolworth, are international. Some are highly specialized, while others are of the bazaar type, selling a wide range of goods. The two main characteristics of this type of shop are:
   (a) One branch is almost identical to the next, with the same shop front, same shop fittings, and same merchandise on sale.
   (b) The branch managers are very strictly controlled from head office, where all important decisions are taken.

   Multiple shops control between 20% and 25% of the retail trade of the Caribbean.
3. *Department stores.* These stores are also known as 'one-stop stores' – they are stores with a wide range of departments under one roof. The first department store was Bon Marché in Paris, opened in 1852. Now every large town in the Caribbean has at least one. To qualify, a store must employ more than 25 persons and sell clothing and four other commodity groups. Department stores attract customers by setting up shop right in the centre of town and by offering a wide choice of good-quality merchandise in luxurious and comfortable surroundings, often with air conditioning and carpeted floors. Despite high running costs, their prices are often competitive because of skilful buying and rapid turnover. Some items are deliberately sold at a loss (as 'loss-leaders') in order to attract people into the store. 'Impulse' purchase items are set out near the doors, to catch customers' eyes as they are on their way to other departments. A typical department store organization is set out in Figure 7.2.
4. *Supermarkets and superettes.* The supermarket originated in the USA in 1914 but did not reach the West Indies till the late 1940s. It is defined as a retail store selling goods by self-service having a floor area of over 200 square metres and with three or more check-out points. A smaller self-service store is known as a superette.

   The supermarkets, even more than other types of shop, rely on a large and rapid turnover to make up for the low prices which attract housewives in their thousands to buy their foodstuffs and other household items such as hardware and detergents. Nearly all super-

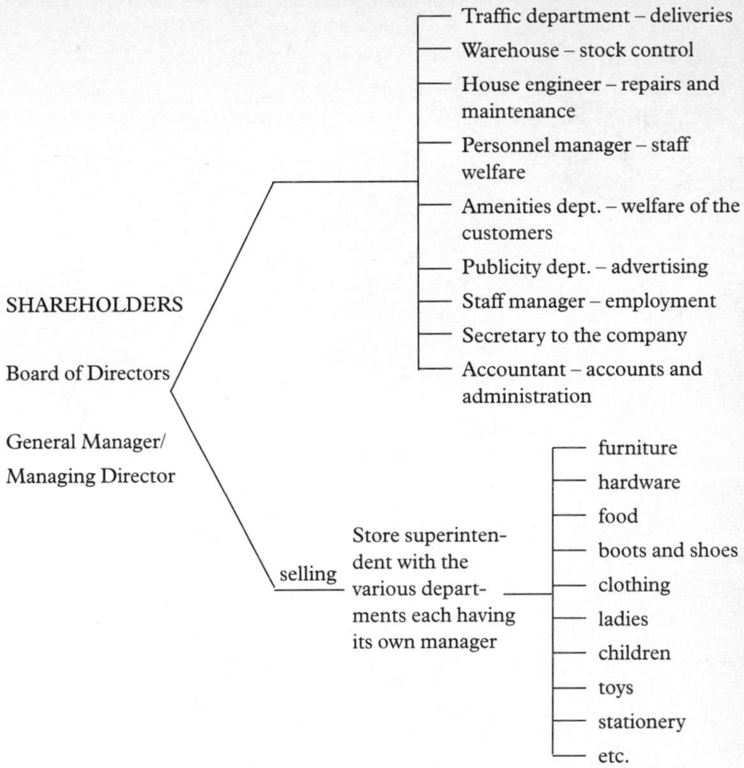

Figure 7.2 Diagram showing the organization of a typical large department store

markets in the Caribbean have a car park and on busy days attendants take purchases to customers' cars. They used to deliver goods to customers' homes, but now this practice is being discontinued.

The main advantages of supermarkets are that, with self-service, a lot of customers can be dealt with in a short time, and the customer can pick and choose without holding others up. Unfortunately, they suffer very badly from theft (also known as pilferage or shoplifting).

5. *Hypermarkets* are very large supermarkets, usually sited out of town, and carrying a wider range of goods.
6. *Discount houses.* These are a recent trend in retail trading, and as yet there are very few in the Caribbean. They sell a limited range of consumer durables (TV sets, refrigerators, etc.) at very low prices, often in converted warehouses, cinemas, etc.
7. *Co-operatives.* These were described in Chapter 2.
8. *Mail order houses.* These are popular in the USA, Canada and the

UK but have never found favour in the Caribbean, perhaps because most islands are so small in area. Customers choose their goods from a catalogue and mail their order with a cheque or postal order. The goods are then supplied by post.

The importance of transport

Transport is the movement of goods and people from one place to another. It is obvious that without transport of some kind, most commercial activities would be impossible. Transport carries raw materials from where they are found, and food from where it is grown, to the factory. It then carries the manufactured goods from the factory to the shop, where the purchaser is able to buy. Transport also takes people to and from their place of work; very few people now live within walking distance of their work.

In the old days, when goods had to be carried by mule or on horseback, or across the sea on small sailing ships, trade was still possible, but transport was very slow and expensive. This meant that as goods had to be carried long distances, they too became very expensive. Some goods, such as fresh meat, fruit and vegetables, could not be carried long distances at all, because they would have gone bad long before they reached their destination. Cheap, efficient and speedy transport is therefore very important in modern commerce, and enables the consumer to be offered a wide range of goods from many countries at reasonable prices. Refrigeration too, combined with good transport, has made it possible to carry perishable goods all over the world.

Types of transport in the Caribbean

Figure 7.3 illustrates the various types of transport used in the Caribbean.

1. *Road transport* is by far the most important form of land transport in the Caribbean, and in most other parts of the world. Its main advantage is that it is very flexible; road vehicles can go almost anywhere, and carry almost any type of load. Goods do not have to be transhipped en route. The main disadvantage is that it creates traffic congestion and causes accidents.

   Goods are carried either by the producers in their own trucks, or by specialized haulage companies. There are also local carriers, particularly in country districts, who take their truck on a regular route on certain days of the week, say to or from the nearest town, collecting and delivering parcels that people have ready for them.

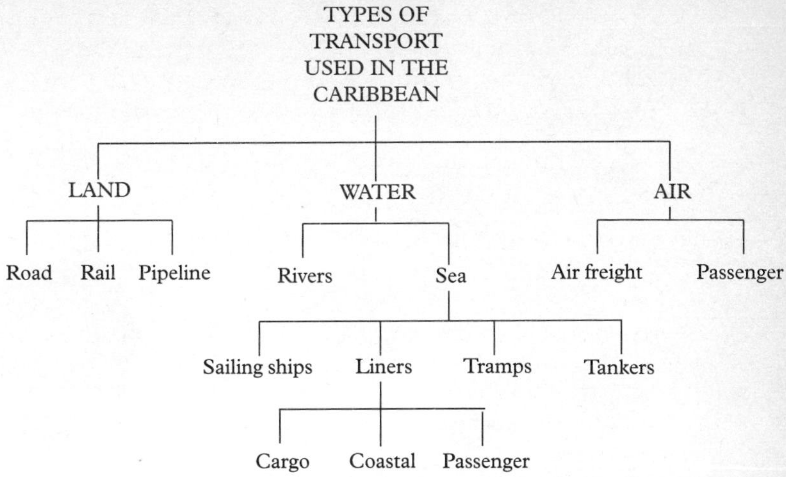

Figure 7.3 Transport used in the Caribbean

2. *Rail transport* has never been very important in the Caribbean. Only Jamaica still has a railway system, which carries mainly passengers, as well as bauxite from the mines to the docks in Kingston. The railways in Barbados, Trinidad and Guyana have all been closed down because they were losing too much money. In larger countries, the railways are still very important for carrying minerals and other bulky items over long distances.
3. *Pipelines* are very suitable for carrying gas or liquids (such as water or oil) in large, regular quantities over a fixed route. They are however expensive to lay down and maintain.
4. *River transport* is also of little importance. Transport by river can be extended and improved by the construction of artificial canals (there are none in the Caribbean).
5. *Sea transport* is very important, particularly in international trade. It is a cheap but slow form of transport. It is very suitable for transporting large, heavy or bulky cargoes such as machinery, vehicles, grain or oil. Many islands depend almost entirely on sea transport for their livelihood. The main types of vessel used are:
   (a) *Sailing ships.* Quite a number are still used in fishing, coastal trade and pleasure boating.
   (b) *Passenger liners.* These are large, specially-built ships that carry passengers, mails and a limited amount of cargo. They used to be the main means of passenger transport between one island and another, and between the Caribbean and the rest of the world, but this traffic has now been lost to the airlines and most

passenger liners in the Caribbean are engaged in pleasure cruising.

(c) *Cargo liners.* These are so called because they carry cargo on a regular 'line' between specified ports, with an advertised timetable of sailings and arrivals. Most shipping lines have a fixed scale of charges of so much per tonne between any two ports. Many liners have now been fitted out to carry containers. Cargo liners ply regularly between the Caribbean and the USA, UK, Europe and Canada. Some may also carry a few passengers.

(d) *Tramps.* These are much the same as cargo liners, but do not sail on a fixed route. They will go wherever there is a cargo to be carried. They are often chartered (hired) for a specific journey. Their rates vary much more than those of liners, being very high when demand is high, and low when demand is low. The liners provide regularity and reliability, while the tramps provide flexibility.

(e) *Tankers* are specially built to carry liquids (such as oil) in bulk. Some tankers are now very large, known as *supertankers.*

(f) *Specially built ships* are increasing. They are specially designed for one specific cargo, such as sugar, bauxite or bananas. There are also refrigerator ships for the transport of perishables.

6. *Air transport* has grown enormously since the end of World War II. It is now the normal means of transporting passengers, mails, newspapers, live animals and highly perishable items over large distances. Air freight is very much more expensive than sea freight but it has the great advantages of speed and flexibility. Aircraft can fly to inland destinations as well as ports, and are not dependent on roads or rivers. Air transport is very suitable for light but valuable items and for such things as urgently needed spare parts. But even buses and trucks can be carried by air if necessary; an all-cargo jumbo jet can carry over 20 tonnes of freight. Much freight (especially mail) is carried on passenger flights, but more and more scheduled all-cargo flights are being run. It is also possible to charter freight aircraft.

Dock and airport facilities

A dock or harbour is the vital connecting point between land and sea transport. (The difference between the two is that a dock is artificially constructed, whereas a harbour is normally a natural feature that has been deepened or provided with protection from the open sea.) Generally the docks and harbours of the Caribbean are well equipped to handle the largest ships likely to use them, but some, such as Port of

Spain, Trinidad, suffer from congestion at busy periods. This causes delay and increases shipping costs.

To operate efficiently, a modern harbour needs the following:

1. Clear, safe access from the sea under all conditions of sea and tide.
2. Ample berthing space.
3. Modern cargo handling equipment, for loading, unloading and transport within the docks.
4. A well-trained and well-managed dock labour force.
5. Efficient and prompt customs inspection facilities.
6. Effective measures against pilfering and smuggling.
7. Adequate storage facilities at or near the docks (not all cargo can be removed immediately it is unloaded). Some of these stores will need to be *in bond* – places where goods can be stored before customs or excise duty has been paid.
8. Quick turn-round for shipping. A ship held up in dock is not earning any money.
9. Bunkering and supply facilities for fuel, water, food, etc.
10. Good rail or road access so that goods can be easily removed from the docks by rail or truck.

In addition, repair facilities will be needed, though not necessarily within the main harbour. These may include a *dry dock,* from which the water can be drained for repairs to the ship's bottom. The exact equipment provided at a dock will depend on the cargo handled; for example, vacuum extractors and elevators will be needed for import and storage of grain.

All the above facilities except the first will also be needed for efficient cargo handling at airports. The airport will, of course, also need runways of adequate length and radio and radar facilities for safe take-off and landing. Because air transport is so important, the Caribbean is well provided with airports. There are large international airports on Antigua, Barbados and Trinidad, at Georgetown in Guyana, at Belize, at Kingston and Montego Bay in Jamaica, and Nassau and Freeport in the Bahamas, as well as dozens of smaller airports.

ACTIVITY

Invent a new product for your company to sell. Prepare and design the packaging and give it a brand name and a logo. Write a report describing the product, the market it is aimed at, and why you have chosen the name and type of packaging.

Think of ways to advertise your product. Draw up an advertisement.

BE A CRITIC

(a) *Packaging:* Choose one good example of packaging and one which you think could be improved. Say why you think this, and give ideas for improvement.

(b) *Advertising:* Describe one advertisement which you think is effective and say why. Describe an advertisement which could be improved and make suggestions for improvement. Say what kind of age-group, type of person each advertisement is aimed at.

(c) *Watch television one evening:* Write down all the advertisements. Say which ones are persuasive, informative, defensive etc.

SELF-REVISION QUESTIONS

1. Explain carefully the different meanings of the word 'market'.
2. Choose a market which you know and state what it sells. Why do you think it was set up in that place?
3. What is the purpose of marketing?
4. Explain the main methods of conducting market research, with the advantages and disadvantages of each.
5. Imagine you are a manufacturer of motor cycles. What steps would you take to decide whether a new model should be produced and what the demand for it is likely to be in your country?
6. If it was decided to import the motor cycles in question 5, how best should they be advertised?
7. Is advertising helpful or harmful? Give reasons for your answer.
8. List the advertising media available in your country.
9. How does advertising differ from public relations?
10. Why is packaging important?
11. List the qualities that a good salesperson should possess.
12. Explain what is meant by the following terms: (a) merchandizing; (b) commission; (c) sales promotion; (d) branding.

8

Business documents

The use of the principal business documents will be illustrated by following through a typical business transaction.

Letter of enquiry

RAM CHAND'S HOTEL

Phone 656-2266

Perseverance Village
Couva, Trinidad, W.I.
March 2, 1998

Messrs S. Arjoon & Sons
28 Prince Street
Port of Spain
Trinidad, W.I.

Reference No. 435 s/a/n

Dear Sirs

In reply to your advertisement appearing in today's issue of 'The News Papers', I should be very happy if you can send me details of prices of vegetables you have to offer.

I operate a small hotel and inn.

Thanks.

Faithfully yours,

Ram Chand

Ram Chand

Figure 8.1 Letter of enquiry

Figure 8.1 shows a typical letter of enquiry. It takes the form of a normal business letter, but the following points should be carefully observed:

1. It must be specific and to the point.
2. It must bear a date and a reference number.
3. If possible it should state definite requirements.

Catalogue and quotation

A *catalogue* is an attractively printed booklet giving a full description of the goods and their prices and the terms and conditions of sale. Catalogues are often printed in colour, with drawings and photographs of the goods that are to be sold. They are very expensive to produce, so some firms may ask their customers to pay for the catalogue when requesting it; the money paid is sometimes deducted from the cost of the first order

QUOTATION

S. ARJOON & SONS LTD

28 Prince Street, Port of Spain
Phone 62-34539
WHOLESALERS, HOTEL SUPPLIERS & SHIPS CHANDLERS

Quotation No. 642 Raj — 7th March 1998

To: Ram Chand's Hotel
Perseverance Village
Couva

Goods	*How sold*	*Price*
Tomatoes	100lb crates	$100.00
Cucumbers	100lb crates	$ 50.00
Carrots	100lb crates	$150.00
Turnips	50lb crates	$ 50.00
Lettuce	100 heads per crate	$ 40.00

Price good until end of April 1998.
Terms: C.O.D.

For and on behalf of
S. Arjoon & Sons

Raj Arjoon

Manager

Figure 8.2 Example of a quotation

sent in. Catalogues are intended for the customer to keep for reference, so that details need not be supplied many times over.

If prices are likely to change often, they may be left out of the catalogue and supplied on a separate *price list*, which may be printed or simply duplicated. This would also be the case if, for example, a firm was trading in several islands and had to charge different prices in each local currency.

When only a few items are requested, or if the goods have to be made specially, the firm will write a letter to the customer giving all the details. This letter is called a *quotation*. It may be on normal notepaper or on a special form, as in Figure 8.2. The quotation should also bear a number which the customer will have to quote when giving his order. The terms and conditions of the proposed sale must also be given.

For building construction and other complex work, the quotation is normally called an *estimate*, because the cost quoted may be varied under certain circumstances. A competitive quotation is a *tender*.

Ram Chand's Hotel receives the quotation, examines it (to see if price, terms, etc. are satisfactory) and decides to place an order (Figure 8.3). If the goods are required immediately, the order could be made by telephone with the written order sent later as confirmation.

ORDER

RAM CHAND'S HOTEL

To: S. Arjoon & Sons Ltd
28 Prince Street
Port of Spain
Trinidad, W.I.

Quotation No. 642 Raj   14th March 1998

Please supply the following C.O.D.:

Quantity	*Particulars*	*Price*	*Total*
2 crates	Tomatoes	$100.00	$200.00
2 crates	Cucumber	$ 50.00	$100.00
1 crate	Lettuce	$ 40.00	$ 40.00

For and on behalf of
Ram Chand's Hotel

Manager

Figure 8.3 Example of an order

Some wholesalers and distributors print order forms which they send to the customer with the catalogue or quotation: in this case, only the blank spaces need be filled in with the details. The quotation from S. Arjoon & Sons requested cash on delivery (COD). This, or cash with order (CWO) is usually the case when dealing with a customer for the first time. As time goes by, an account may be opened with Arjoons by Ram Chand's Hotel so that goods can be supplied on credit. To do this, Arjoons may request of Ram Chand's Hotel a bank *reference* (a statement from a bank on their credit-worthiness).

The invoice

The goods are now sent to the buyer with an accompanying *invoice* (Figure 8.4). The invoice gives full details of the goods sent, conditions of sale and delivery. It also shows how much is being charged. The seller always keeps a copy of the invoice for his own records, but extra copies are sometimes needed. A copy packed in the parcel with the goods is known as a *packing note*. A copy handed to the truck driver on which he gets a signature as proof of delivery, is called a *delivery note*. If a copy is sent to the buyer before the goods, it is known as an *advice note*. Invoices usually carry the abbreviation E. & O.E., meaning 'errors and omissions

INVOICE

S. ARJOON & SONS LTD

28 Prince Street, Port of Spain
Phone 62-34539
WHOLESALERS, HOTEL SUPPLIERS & SHIPS CHANDLERS

Quotation No. 642 Raj — 21st March 1998

To: Ram Chand's Hotel
Perseverance Village
Couva

2 crates	Tomatoes @ $100.00 per crate	200.00
2 crates	Cucumbers @ $50.00 per crate	100.00
1 crate	Lettuce @ $40.00 per crate	40.00
		$340.00

E&OE

Figure 8.4 Example of an invoice

excepted'. It indicates that the seller reserves the right to make any adjustments that are necessary if there is a mistake on the invoice.

Proforma invoices are sometimes used (*pro forma* is a Latin phrase meaning 'for formality's sake') in the following circumstances:

1. To show the buyer exactly what he would have to pay (in place of a quotation).
2. When payment is required in advance.
3. When goods are sent to an agent to sell on commission (to tell him how much he should charge for them).
4. When goods are sent through the customs free of charge, so that the customs have a statement of the goods and their value.
5. To accompany goods sent out on approval, so that the buyer knows how much to pay if he keeps the goods.

The receipt

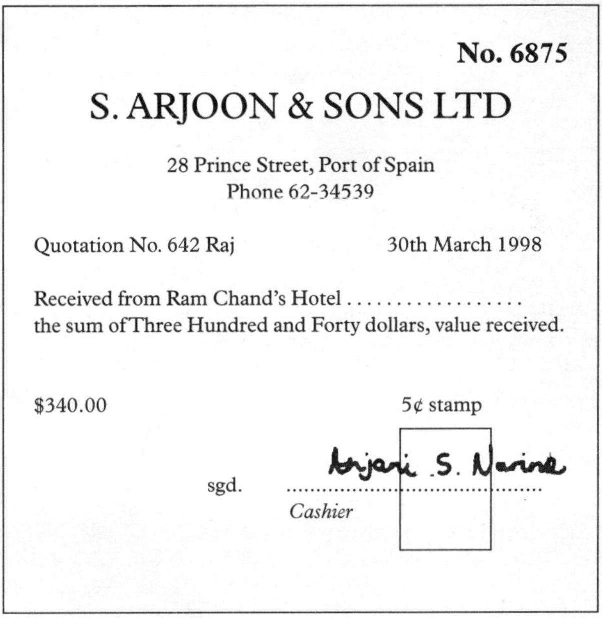
No. 6875

S. ARJOON & SONS LTD

28 Prince Street, Port of Spain
Phone 62-34539

Quotation No. 642 Raj 30th March 1998

Received from Ram Chand's Hotel ....
the sum of Three Hundred and Forty dollars, value received.

$340.00 5¢ stamp

sgd. Anjani S. Naina
Cashier

Figure 8.5 Example of a receipt

If the goods are received in good condition, the customer will have to pay for them, as described in Chapter 5. It is customary to issue *a receipt* (Figure 8.5) as proof of payment, although when payment is made by cheque a receipt is not necessary, because clearance of the cheque through the banking system is accepted as proof of payment. In most countries receipts for amounts $5 or over must bear a postage stamp (5¢ or 10¢). Receipts are usually written out on forms in numbered receipt books; either they are made out in duplicate with carbon paper, or a counterfoil is provided.

Credit note

Sometimes a mistake is made and the customer is entitled to a refund:

1. The goods may be damaged or defective.
2. There may have been a shortage, or some item left out altogether.
3. The wrong price may have been charged.
4. Trade discount may have been omitted, or given at too low a rate.
5. There may have been a mistake in the arithmetic.
6. The goods may not have been ordered at all.

These mistakes are corrected by the supplier issuing a *credit note,* which has the effect of cancelling all or part of the debt established by the invoice. A credit note looks very like an invoice and to avoid confusion it is usually printed or typed in red.

If too little has been charged, the mistake is corrected by the supplier issuing a *debit note* – in effect, a supplementary invoice.

Statement of account

At regular intervals, usually once a month, the seller sends his credit account customers a statement of purchases and payments since the accounts were last balanced. The balance shown on the statement of account is the amount owing by the customer.

Consignment note

When goods are handed to a carrier, trucking company or railway to deliver, a *consignment note* is made out. Most transport companies have their own specially printed form for the purpose. This sets out the names and addresses of the consignor (sender) and consignee (recipient), the nature (and often the weight) of the goods, the freight charge, and who is responsible for damage in transit. The sender usually receives a duplicate copy from the transport company for their records; this also acts as a receipt for the goods.

If goods are carried at 'owner's risk', the consignor may take out an insurance policy to cover himself against loss or damage in transit.

International business transactions

As can be imagined, international business transactions are very much more complicated than those in home trade. All the documents used in home trade are also used in international trade, but extra documents are also required.

First, the means of payment need to be established. The risk of default is much greater, yet it is impossible to ask for cash or a normal bank cheque.

1. A proforma invoice can be sent as a request for payment in advance. The customer then remits the money by means of a *bank draft* drawn on a bank in the seller's country.
2. If the buyer is unwilling to pay until he is sure that the goods have been shipped, he can establish (through his own bank) a *letter of credit* with a bank in the seller's country. This bank then pays the seller when he can produce the shipping documents (see below). A letter of credit may carry a time limit, after which it *expires*, and it may be *revocable* or *irrevocable*. A revocable letter of credit can be cancelled at any time.
3. A period of credit may be offered to the customer by accepting a letter of credit which is payable a certain period after the shipping documents have been presented.
4. The goods can be shipped without advance payment, but the shipping documents are sent to a bank in the customer's country with instructions not to hand them over until payment has been made. This provides some protection to both parties, since the customer is protected against delays in delivery, but cannot claim the goods from the shipping line without the documents.
5. Goods can be supplied to trusted customers on the *open account* system; they are supplied on credit exactly as in a home market transaction, except that the period of credit is usually longer. Payment will be made by bank draft, as in (1).
6. The seller can send the buyer a *bill of exchange* (Figure 8.6) for the amount due. When the buyer accepts this, by signing his name across its face, he has made a legally binding obligation to pay the amount of the bill on the date specified (a period of 3–6 months' credit is often allowed). This is not a 100% guarantee of payment, but a bill is easier to enforce than an ordinary trading debt, and a bank may be willing to *discount* it (buy it for slightly less than its face value). It must be emphasized that bills of exchange are now rarely used in this way.

It is also necessary to establish the currency in which payment is

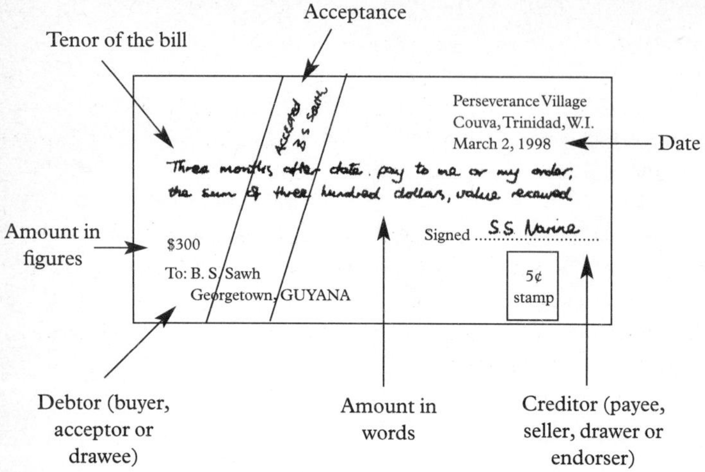

Figure 8.6 Bill of exchange

to be made. This can make quite a difference if the rate of exchange alters. It is usual for the seller to invoice in his own currency, but he may wish to specify the amount to be paid in the buyer's currency, or in another well-known currency such as sterling or US dollars.

Bill of lading and other shipping documents

The *bill of lading* is a crucial document for sending goods by ship. It is both a contract for carriage and a document of title. It is made out by the exporter or his shipping agent at the port at which the goods are taken on board, and covers the following information: the type, quantity and value of the goods; the distinguishing marks on the crates or bales (used so that they can be easily recognized at a distance); the name of the exporter; the name and address of the recipient; the number of boxes or crates; the name of the ship; and the ports of loading and destination.

When the goods are loaded at the port or dock, they are checked against the bill of lading. Any damage or discrepancy must be recorded and noted in the bill of lading before it is signed. The captain of the ship or his agent will sign the bill to certify that the goods listed have been received for shipment; it thus acts as a valid receipt. One signed copy is retained by the sender; at least two further signed copies are sent to the recipient (or a bank), as without these the goods cannot be claimed from the shipping line on arrival. The captain of the ship will also retain a copy, and from this he makes up his *ship's manifest* (a list of the cargo carried). The shipping company is only responsible for loss or damage if this is caused by its own, or its employees' neglect. All other losses, such as from fire or storm, must be covered by insurance.

Most goods imported are subject to customs duty. Before he can clear goods through customs, an importer must complete a *customs entry* detailing the goods, on which duty is assessed and paid. The customs then issue an *out of charge note* as an authority to the port officials to release the goods.

More and more goods are being carried in containers. Goods within a container are covered by a *standard shipping note,* which gives instructions to the agent who receives and opens the container at the destination as to who should receive the various goods. One note is made out for each consignee.

Air waybill

This is the standard document used to accompany all air freight shipments. It is also known as an 'air consignment note' and in fact it contains much the same information as an ordinary consignment note. It is filled in by the sender or his agent before handing the goods to the airline. Because air transport is so international, an identical layout of air waybill is used by all airlines.

There is one important difference between an air waybill and bill of lading: an air waybill is not a document of title. That is to say, a shipping company will not hand over goods except to the possessor of a signed bill of lading, but the airline will simply hand over the goods to the consignee named on the air waybill. This is because air transport is so fast that the goods would normally arrive before an air waybill could be sent by the consignor.

Miscellaneous means of payment

Most of the means of payment of importance to business people have already been covered in Chapter 5 and earlier in this chapter. However, there are others which are sometimes used in business and which are also important for the private citizen.

1. *Postal orders* provide a convenient means of paying small amounts. They can be bought at post offices in a variety of denominations (values). If there is no order available for the exact amount required, the few extra cents can be made up by sticking postage stamps on the order. Besides the value of the order itself, the purchaser must also pay a small fee (called *poundage*), which will be higher on larger value orders. The order is stamped by the post office clerk when it is

sold, the customer fills in the name of the payee and (for extra security) the name of the post office at which it is to be paid, and completes and detaches the counterfoil, which should be kept carefully – if the order is lost in the post, the counterfoil must be produced before the post office will consider any claims. The recipient signs the order and presents it at the post office named on it, and receives the money. The paying clerk stamps the order a second time to prevent its re-use. If a postal order is crossed, it can only be paid into a bank account like a cheque.

2. *Money orders* are used for larger payments than postal orders; because of the large sums of money involved, the procedure is more complicated. The sender must fill out an application form giving the full name and address of the payee. After paying the sum due, the sender transmits the receipted form to the payee. Meanwhile the issuing post office will have sent the order itself to the paying post office. When the payee goes he must present the receipt and some means of identification. The two halves of the order are then matched up and the money paid over.
3. *Telegraphic money orders* operate in the same way as ordinary money orders, except that the payment advice is sent by telegram. The sender must pay the cost of the telegram in addition to the money order fee. They are thus more expensive, but payment can be made much more quickly.
4. *International money orders* are also available (subject to control regulations).
5. *Promissory notes* (see Figure 8.7) differ from bills of exchange insofar as they only have two parties to them – the person who promises to pay, and the person to whom the promise is made. It is, in other words, a direct promise by the person writing it out to pay, and not an order to a third person to pay over the amount. Like bills of exchange, promissory notes are legally enforceable, and they can be transferred from one holder to another. Also, a promissory note is a *negotiable instrument*; this means that anyone receiving it 'in good faith' receives a good title (i.e. a legal right) to it, whether the person who gave it to him had any right to it or not. Negotiability, in this legal sense, should not be confused with transferability.

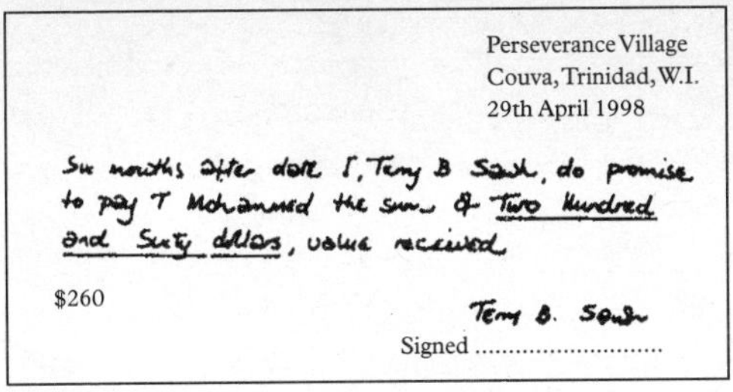

Perseverance Village
Couva, Trinidad, W.I.
29th April 1998

Six months after date I, Terry B Sawh, do promise to pay T Mohammed the sum of Two Hundred and Sixty dollars, value received.

$260

Terry B. Sawh
Signed ....

Figure 8.7 Promissory note

ACTIVITIES

1. Go to a shipping or freight company and ask for copies of as many different documents as possible. Familiarize yourself with them. Make a display of them.
2. Imagine you are exporting 1,000 copies of an album recorded by a local singer to a music shop in the USA. Make up names for the singer and the album, for your own business, and for the shop you are sending them to. Draw a flow chart to show the documents you will need, in the right order, saying who is sending them where.

SELF-REVISION QUESTIONS

1. All the following are used to inform customers about a firm's products. Say when each might be used:
   (a) Catalogue.
   (b) Price list.
   (c) Quotation.
   (d) Tender.
2. What other means does a firm have of giving information about its products besides those listed in Question 1?
3. Give *three* reasons why a firm might ask for cash with order.
4. List the items normally found on an invoice.
5. What is a proforma invoice? When is it used?
6. Make out an invoice for the following consignment: The Universal Trading Company of Water Lane, Kingston are selling two dozen 1-litre cans of white supergloss paint at $5 per litre, plus 401-litre cans of cream emulsion at $4.50 per litre to Sunset Stores Ltd of Spanish Town. Trade discount is 20%,

carriage of $12.50 is to be charged, and UTC are prepared to offer a cash discount of 2½% for payment within ten days. The consignment is to go off next Monday.

7. One of the cases containing a dozen cans of gloss paint (see Question 6) bursts in transit and three cans are lost. State what action would be taken as a result of this mishap.
8. What is a consignment note? How does it differ from a delivery note?
9. Why do businesses usually supply their trade customers on credit, despite the risk of bad debts?
10. X Ltd in Trinidad wishes to sell goods to Y Ltd in Guyana. X is not sure of Y's credit worthiness, but Y refuses to pay until the goods have been delivered to Georgetown docks in good condition. What means of payment would you recommend?
11. Name *two* essential differences between a bill of lading and an air waybill.
12. Which means of payment would be most suitable:
    (a) To pay $1,000 to another business in the same island?
    (b) To pay $1,000 to a supplier in the USA?
    (c) To pay $50 by post to someone without a bank account?
    (d) To pay rent every month to your landlord?
13. What is the difference between a bill of exchange and a promissory note?
14. Describe the precautions you might take to ensure that a postal order cannot be cashed by a thief.

9

Money, capital and the financial sector

Money

Trade in earliest times was conducted by means of *barter,* i.e. simple exchange of one set of goods for another. This was not very convenient, for the following reasons:

1. The other party might not have anything you wanted to give you in exchange.
2. The other party's goods might not be available in convenient units or of the right value. For example, it would be no good offering a cow in exchange for half a dozen eggs; a cow cannot be subdivided until she is dead!
3. It could be very difficult to establish the relative value of the goods being exchanged; there was no common measure of value.

Barter has now virtually died out, although it still occurs very occasionally, for example among close friends or country people who will give each other surplus produce; the recipient knows that he will be expected to 'give' something in return fairly soon.

Money as we know it today was invented by the Greeks about 650 BC. Because barter was so inconvenient, the use of money quickly spread throughout the civilized world. We usually think of money as coins and bank notes, but in fact other things have been used as money from time to time – cattle, cowrie shells, even cigarettes. The first money consisted of gold and silver coins, and their value was that of the weight of gold or silver that they contained. They were more convenient than gold or silver bars or jewellery, because each coin carried a characteristic design and its weight (and therefore its value) was exactly known; it did not have to be weighed, and its value calculated, each time goods were bought or sold.

Each gold or silver coin had quite a high value, and coins of smaller value were soon needed. These were struck in a cheaper metal, bronze, and unlike gold or silver coins, their value did not depend on the value of the bronze they contained; their value lay in the fact that the government undertook to exchange so many bronze coins for one silver one. They were *token* coins; they had little value in themselves – their value lay in what could be bought with them, or obtained for them. Their chief disadvantage was that they were easy to forge until sophisticated, modern coin-making machinery was invented.

The next step forward took place as a result of the development of the modern banking system in the eighteenth and nineteenth centuries. Rich men and merchants found it inconvenient to carry around with them and have at home large quantities of gold and silver coins. They began to deposit their gold and silver with bankers for safe keeping. In exchange the bankers issued receipts, which people found were acceptable as a means of payment. The next step was the issue of 'bank notes' (as they came to be called) for specific denominations (such as $1, $5, etc.), but still these were sometimes refused outside the town of issue, and from time to time small banks closed and could not honour their notes. So finally the Central Banks (in effect the government) took over the issue of bank notes. Nearly all high-value gold and silver coins have now been withdrawn, so today we have an entirely token currency.

What is it that makes money so useful and gives it acceptability? The essential characteristics of money are as follows:

1. It is *universally acceptable* because its value is ultimately guaranteed by the government. Just occasionally, as in certain South American countries, the monetary system breaks down, there is rampant inflation and money loses its value so fast that people are no longer prepared to accept it. But this is very unusual.
2. It acts as a *medium of exchange.*
3. It acts as a *measure of value.* If asked what your house is worth, you would quote a specific sum in dollars.
4. It acts as a *store of value.* Money is compact. It is easily stored and carried around. It does not rot or get eaten by insects (like wood), or rust (like iron), or need feeding or die (like animals).
5. It is *easily divisible* – payment can be made to the nearest cent.
6. It is *readily convertible.* It can be quickly converted into goods or other forms of wealth, unlike other valuable articles such as houses or jewellery, which can be difficult to sell for their full value at short notice. (This convertibility may not apply outside the country of issue.)
7. It acts as a *standard of deferred payment.* This means that without money, loans would be very difficult to negotiate, it is money that enables one to specify the amount of interest and repayment.

The importance of these characteristics can be illustrated by testing them on other things which are not money. For instance, a cheque fails on the first test – it is not universally acceptable. Gold bars would fail the fifth and sixth tests.

Commercial banks

The primary functions of all banks are twofold: the acceptance of money on deposit (for safe keeping or because of the interest offered) and making advances (loans or overdrafts). The bank makes its profit out of the difference between what it pays in interest on deposits and what it charges in interest in advances.

There are many different types of bank, but the commonest is the *clearing bank*. Branches of these banks are to be found in all major towns. Some operate only within one or two islands; others, such as Barclays and the Royal Bank of Canada, operate world-wide. The main services offered by these banks are:

1. *Current accounts*, also known as *cheque accounts*. Private citizens as well as businessmen place money they may need at short notice in this account for safe keeping and to use the bank's cheque facilities. No interest is usually paid on current accounts, but customers draw cheques on the account; these are instructions to the bank to pay a specified amount of money from the account to a specified third party. The cheque is sent or given to the recipient, who pays it in (with a paying-in or deposit slip) to his own bank, which then collects the money from the bank of the person who wrote the cheque and credits it to the recipient's account. An account holder will also write a cheque (made out to 'self or 'cash') to draw cash from his account.

   There are two main types of cheque:
   (a) *Open cheques*. These can be exchanged for cash by the payee (or bearer, if made out to 'cash' or 'bearer') if presented at the branch of the bank on which they were drawn.
   (b) *Crossed cheques*. These have two vertical lines printed or drawn across the face (as in Figure 9.1). The recipient can only pay the cheque into his bank account; he cannot draw cash. Crossing a cheque provides some protection against thieves. The drawer can *open the crossing* by writing 'Please pay cash' with his initials between the two lines; it then becomes an open cheque.
2. *Deposit accounts*. There are several variations, such as *savings accounts* and *fixed deposit accounts*, but the main differences from current accounts are:

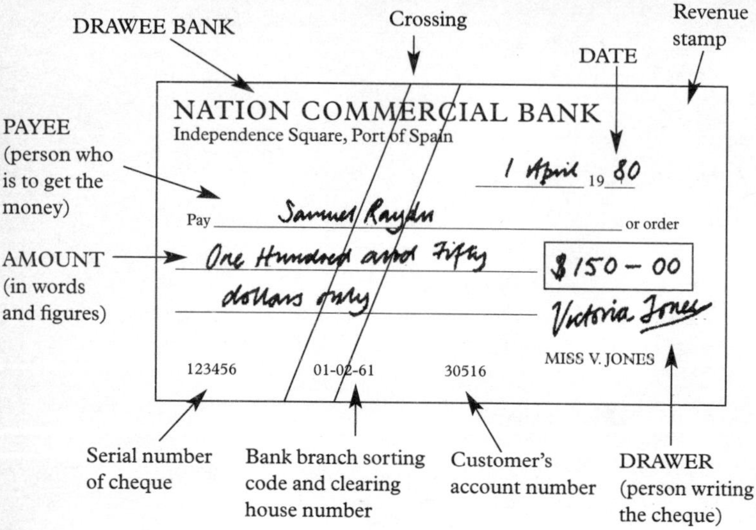

Figure 9.1 Essential features of a cheque

(a) Interest is paid.
(b) Cheques cannot be drawn on the account.
(c) Money or cheques can be paid into the account at any time, but the bank is entitled to notice (usually seven days) before money can be drawn out.

3. *Night safe facilities.* These are particularly important for shop-keepers, who may want to bank their takings long after the banks have closed. The cash is placed in a special bag with a *paying-in slip* (see Figure 9.2) and placed in a special aperture in the wall of the bank, where it falls into the bank's night safe. The cash is counted, the account credited and the receipted counterfoil and bag collected, when the bank reopens.
4. *Safe deposit facilities.* For a small fee, customers can deposit valuables such as jewellery, silver and share certificates with the bank for safe keeping. They are either placed in a large envelope in the bank's own safe, or in an individual safe-deposit strong-box to which the customer is given a key.
5. *Money changers,* or *cash dispensers.* A few banks have special electronic machines which enable customers to draw limited amounts of cash when the bank is closed.

NATION COMMERCIAL BANK

Credit ....

....

Account No. ....

Deposited by ....

....

Date .... 19.......

Notes:	$	¢
× $100 × $20 × $10 × $5 × $1		
Total notes Total of cheques (put list of all cheques on the other side)		
Total Coins		
NET DEPOSIT		

NATION COMMERCIAL BANK

Credit ....

....

Account No. ....

Deposited by ....

....

Date .... 19.......

Notes:	$	¢
× $100 × $20 × $10 × $5 × $1		
Total notes Total of cheques (put list of all cheques on the other side)		
Total Coins		
NET DEPOSIT		

Figure 9.2 Paying-in or deposit slip (current account)

6. *Foreign exchange.* Those travelling abroad can obtain foreign currency notes from their bank. The bank will also arrange payment of bills due to foreign suppliers; in many cases they will also attend to the formalities of obtaining exchange control permission or import licences from the Central Bank, if these are required.
7. *Travellers' cheques.* When travelling away from home, citizens' personal cheques are seldom accepted, because shopkeepers and hotel-keepers are uncertain whether they will be honoured. Banks therefore issue travellers' cheques (in local or foreign currency)

which are easy to cash because payment is guaranteed by the issuing bank.

When travelling within the Caribbean, only special Caribbean Travellers' Cheques will be issued to the traveller, by agreement among the governments of the Caribbean. The cheques come in various denominations, each having a different colour for easy identification. Such a traveller will not be sold any other type of travellers' cheque or foreign currency such as US dollars or British pounds.

8. *Bank drafts.* These look like cheques, but are drawn by one bank on another, or by one branch on another. They can be purchased by customers when they have to pay specific sums and a personal cheque would not be acceptable. Payment is guaranteed by the bank.
9. *Letters of credit.* These are often used by businesses which wish to buy goods abroad but which are not well known to the foreign supplier. The bank establishes a credit of the sum required at another bank in the supplier's country, which is then paid to the supplier on production of proof of dispatch of the goods. They are called letters of credit, because the advice to the recipient that the credit has been established is in the form of a letter.
10. *Transfers.* These are means of transferring money from one bank account to another without the use of cheques. There are three main types:
    (a) *Credit transfers.* The customer fills in a slip for each payment (giving details of branch, account no. etc.) and signs one cheque for the total of all the payments. The transfer is then effected through the banks' clearing house system.
    (b) *Mail transfers.* These are used for overseas payments. The advice of transfer is sent by post and may take a long time to arrive unless an *air mail transfer* (AMT) is specified.
    (c) *Telegraphic transfer* (TT). Used for urgent payments overseas. The advice is sent by telegram or telex.
11. *Standing orders*, or *bankers orders*. On receipt of signed instructions the bank will make regular payments of a fixed amount every month, quarter or year. Useful for rent, subscriptions, etc., which might otherwise be overlooked. It is also possible for customers to order the bank to pay whatever sum a creditor demands: this is known as a *direct debit*.
12. *Loans.* Banks are always willing to consider requests for loans if the customer can provide adequate security (see later in this chapter). The loan is for a specific period and must be repaid when the time is up, or by instalments. The interest must be paid throughout, even if some of the money has been repaid, and the true rate of interest

charged may therefore be considerably higher than that quoted.

13. *Overdrafts.* Selected customers may be given permission to overdraw their current account (i.e., take out more than they have put in) for a specified period and up to a specified limit. Interest is only charged on the amount overdrawn. Overdrafts are an important source of short-term finance for businessmen. However, if a customer overdraws on his account without permission, his cheques will not be paid (honoured) by the bank; such cheques are known as 'bouncing' (dishonoured) cheques.
14. *Credit references.* A bank will obtain from another bank an opinion on the credit-worthiness of a client with whom a customer is thinking of opening an account.
15. *Financial advice.* Many small-business managers turn to their bank manager for financial advice, particularly on ways of raising fresh capital.
16. *Executor and trustee work.* Many banks have special departments to administer estates of those who have died, and to look after trust funds (funds established for the benefit of a third party, such as a young child). Fees are charged according to the work involved.

Personal budgeting

It is not wise for anyone to spend all his income immediately. If he does not put some by, here are some of the expenses he may have difficulty in meeting:

- New clothes for special occasions, babies, children, etc.
- Electricity and telephone bills.
- Car repairs, taxation and insurance.
- Rent and rates.
- Insurance premiums.
- School books and uniforms.
- Visits to sick relatives, funerals, etc.

The only solution is to work out how much each of these items is likely to cost when the bills come in, and to ensure that the money is available by careful planning and saving.

It is always wise to open a bank current account. Not only does it make paying bills easier if it can be done by cheque, but spare cash is much safer in the bank and the bank sends out from time to time statements of account, which provide a convenient record of all the money paid out and put into the bank. It is much easier to estimate the size of the next electricity bill, for instance, if you know how much it was last time.

For longer-term saving, it is better if your money is earning some interest. There are several systems to choose from:

1. *Savings account* at a commercial bank. It takes as little as $1 to open this type of account. Interest paid ranges between 2% and 5%, paid quarterly, half-yearly or yearly, and is credited to the account. Money can be paid in at any time by anybody by completing a deposit slip, but money can only be drawn out by the account-holder completing a withdrawal form or debit slip. The customer receives a pass book in which all transactions are recorded. An additional advantage of this type of account is that bank managers tend to look more favourably on applications for loans from customers who have a good saving record with their bank.
2. *Post Office Savings Bank.* This operates very much like a savings account, but deposits and withdrawals can be made at any post office in the country (not at postal agencies), and the rate of interest is very seldom changed – the exact amount varies from country to country. Only limited amounts can be withdrawn on demand; for larger sums notice must be given on a form obtainable at post offices.
3. *Credit unions.* These are associations of workers pooling their savings into a common loan fund, from which loans are made to members at low rates of interest for approved 'provident and productive purposes'; these might be things like medical and dental bills, purchase of household articles, education fees, school books or house repairs. Each member receives 'interest' on his contribution in the form of a share of the union's yearly earnings. Operations of credit unions are closely supervised by the government.
4. *Fixed deposit accounts.* These are suitable for those who have spare cash that they are certain not to need for some while. Fixed deposit accounts earn better interest than savings accounts; the greater the amount of money and the longer the period of deposit, the higher the rate of interest. Sums are deposited for a fixed term; if they are withdrawn before the term expires, the customer suffers a considerable loss of interest.
5. *Deposit accounts.* These are designed for quite large sums of money and are mainly of interest to businesses with a temporary surplus. The interest is higher than on savings accounts.
6. *Savings at finance companies.* There are now many such companies in the Caribbean. They pay very high rates of interest. To encourage savings, they give gift vouchers encashable at certain stores. Some also give the interest in advance – as soon as the deposit is made.

7. *Trust companies.* These are subsidiary companies of commercial banks (they sometimes combine with other banks or with large companies). They pay a higher rate of interest than commercial banks. Like finance companies, they only accept fixed deposits for a long term.

Many people find it easier to save if they sign a standing order to transfer so much every month from their current account to one of these savings media. Some employers will make a deduction from wages, if requested, and pay this into a savings account each month.

An important means of saving for a long-term future is provided by *life insurance.* By paying a regular premium every month or quarter, they earn a lump sum payment when they retire, which can be converted into a pension. Should they die before reaching retirement age, a lump sum payment is made to their widow or family.

Sources and types of capital

Some of the forms of capital used by businesses have already been discussed in Chapter 2. It is now time to consider how business people raise capital when they cannot provide it themselves from their own savings or accumulated profits, or find friends who are prepared to go into partnership with them. It is usual to divide capital into short-term and long-term capital.

Short-term capital is that required to finance day-to-day business transactions. The businessman will expect to repay it within a short period – certainly within a year – from sales income, profits, or another source of capital. The main sources of short-term capital are:

1. *Loans.* Usually arranged through a bank, which will want to be satisfied that it is going to get its money back, i.e. that the business is being soundly run. A special form of loan is the *bridging loan*, required, say, when a shopkeeper has to buy a new shop before he can sell his old one. Such loans carry a heavy interest charge, and are taken out for as short a period as possible.
2. *Overdrafts.*
3. *Credit from suppliers.* Many goods are supplied to manufacturers and retailers on credit – that is to say, they do not have to be paid for immediately. By that time it may be possible to sell them for cash.

The main sources of external *long-term capital* are *shares* and *debentures.* These are described in the section on limited companies in Chapter 2. It is important for a public 'quoted' company to arrange for its shares and debentures to be quoted (traded) on a *stock exchange*: otherwise shareholders will not be able to sell their shares easily and may be very reluctant to invest. There are stock exchanges in many large cities of the non-communist world which trade in shares and debentures of local companies as well as government securities; members of the public wishing to buy or sell shares approach a stockbroker who will negotiate for the shares on the exchange on their behalf, charging a fee called *brokerage*. There are stock exchanges in Jamaica, Barbados and Trinidad. The one in Trinidad is known as the Trinidad and Tobago Stock Exchange and is found at 65 Independence Square, Port of Spain.

Companies and firms that cannot issue shares to the public may find it difficult to raise long-term finance. Banks are reluctant to make loans on a long-term basis, but may occasionally do so. Other sources of long-term finance which may be available are:

1. *The Caribbean Development Bank.* This institution lends money to farmers and manufacturers at a low rate of interest to assist them in purchasing fertilizers and seeds and in setting up factories. (The CDB also lends money to governments to provide roads and harbours and irrigation projects.)
2. *Loans from insurance companies.* These are sometimes prepared to lend money to buy land, construct buildings, etc. and then let the farmers or industrialists buy an insurance policy on instalments, which, when it matures, provides enough money for them to repay the money outright. This is called an *endowment mortgage.*
3. *Sale and leaseback.* A business which already owns its premises but is short of working capital may sell the premises to a bank or finance company and then lease them back for an annual rental.

Collateral and security

No bank or other financial institution will make a loan of any size without adequate security. This is something which can be sold if the borrower fails to repay the loan. The following are usually acceptable as security.

1. Mortgages or title deeds to land or buildings.
2. Life insurance policies.
3. Stock and share certificates. The bank will of course ensure that the shares are in reputable companies and not likely to go down in value.
4. Gold, silver, jewellery, works of art and other valuables.

The items do not become the bank's property, but for all except the last the bank manager gets the customer to sign a *letter of hypothecation* which grants the bank the right to sell the asset left as security if the loan is not repaid.

However, competition for business between banks can be very keen and they may occasionally make a loan to a trusted customer without demanding the deposit of security; the loan is then *unsecured.* Collateral means, in practice, the same as security, and is the usual term for security in the USA.

Principles of insurance and assurance

It is possible for people and firms to safeguard themselves against most everyday risks by paying a small regular sum (the *premium*) and receiving a sum by way of compensation if and when the risk happens. When it is certain that the 'risk' will occur at some time, and the only doubtful thing is *when,* the procedure is known as *assurance.* An example is one's death. If the doubtful factor is *if* it will happen, such as fire and theft, then it is known as *insurance.*

This principle can be illustrated from the following example. Suppose on an island there are 750 houses, each of which would cost $50,000 to rebuild. An insurance company decides that, on average, only one house will burn down a year, and arranges insurance for all the householders. Clearly it must raise at least $50,000 a year to cover likely claims, so it decides to charge an insurance premium of 0.2% of the sum insured (i.e. 0.2% × $50,000 = $100 a year for each householder). This will raise750 × $100 = $75,000 a year. If it pays out $50,000 in claims, it will have $25,000 left to cover administrative costs and profit.

There are some special insurance terms which need to be understood. When a person requires insurance, he fills out a *proposal* form; if this is accepted by the insurance company, the company issues an insurance *policy,* a document which sets out the terms and conditions of the contract between the *insurer* (the insurance company) and the *insured* (the policy-holder) – it states the *risk* (the thing or person that is being insured), the *event* or *contingency* (the thing which is being insured against), the *sum insured* (the maximum amount of compensation payable) and the *premium* (the amount the policy-holder will have to pay). If the thing insured against happens, the policy-holder makes a *claim* (usually on a special form supplied by the insurance company), and if it is a big one, the company may send a *loss adjuster* to check the damage (known to the insurance company as the *loss*).

Types of insurance and assurance

There are three main types of insurance and assurance. Companies may provide only one type.

1. *Life assurance.* There are three main sub-divisions:
   (a) *Term assurance.* The sum assured is paid if the assured person dies within the term of (period covered by) the policy.
   (b) *Whole-life assurance.* The sum assured is paid when the assured person dies, whenever this may be.
   (c) *Endowment assurance.* The sum assured is paid at the end of a specified period (often a man's date of retirement), or on death, if earlier. Many private pension schemes are based on endowment assurance. This is the most popular type of life assurance. It provides valuable protection for a person's children and dependents if he or she dies unexpectedly.

   Some life assurance companies also offer *with-profits policies*. Under these policies, there is a guaranteed sum payable on death or maturity but this is increased from time to time by the company ploughing back part of the profits it makes to buy extra insurance cover for the policy-holder. Naturally with-profits policies cost more than ordinary contracts but they provide some protection against the value of the sum insured being reduced in real terms by inflation.
2. *Accident insurance.* This can cover not only accidents but all types of injury or sickness in people, and loss, damage or theft of goods or animals. Unlike life assurance, payment is *only* made to compensate for the exact amount of loss or expense incurred. It is usually necessary to take out a separate policy for each risk, but more and more companies are now offering comprehensive insurance 'packages' to the public. Some of the most common types of insurance cover are:
   - House buildings and contents – fire, storm and theft.
   - Motor vehicles (including damage to other vehicles and drivers*).
   - Health and accident.
   - Employers' (damage caused by or to workers).
   - Industrial premises and equipment – this may include loss of profits while damage is being repaired.

   (Those marked * are compulsory.)

   Nearly all governments now provide health, retirement and unemployment insurance for their citizens (see Chapter 9).
3. *Marine insurance.* This covers insurance of ships and their cargos and, more recently, of aircraft. It is treated as a separate branch of insurance because it is so specialized.

Insurance contracts

The law makes special provisions on the enforcement of insurance contracts (policies). The most important are:

1. *Utmost good faith* (also known by its Latin name, *uberrima fides*). The person taking out the insurance must disclose all matters concerning the risk to be insured, even if not specifically asked to do so. Failure to do so may render the contract invalid and mean that a claim will not be met.
2. *Insurable interest.* This means that what one is going to insure must be one's own, or that one must have a legitimate interest in it. It is insurable interest that distinguishes insurance from wagers and gambling, which will not be upheld by the courts. Thus a woman may take out life insurance on her husband's life, because she has a legitimate interest in his continuing to live, but a policy on the life of Michael Jackson would not be allowable. One may insure against losing one's purse, but not against the West Indies losing a test match.
3. *Indemnity.* The insurance company is only obliged to pay enough to reinstate (restore) an article to its previous condition. Thus if a five-year-old car is stolen, the insurance company will only pay its market value, not the cost of a brand new one. (Recently some insurance companies have begun to offer *replacement value* policies for a higher premium.)
4. *Average.* This word has a special meaning in insurance. It means in effect that if your house is worth $50,000 and you only insure it for $25,000 (half its value), then only the same proportion will be paid on any claims for damage, even if within the sum insured. If minor damage was suffered, costing $5,000, only $2,500 would be paid. This rule is very important. In times of inflation it is very easy to insure items unwittingly for less than their full value.

Central banks

Most countries have a Central Bank, though it may carry a different name (in the USA the Federal Reserve Bank, in Britain the Bank of England). Its functions are as follows:

1. It acts as banker to the government. It receives the proceeds of taxation, pays for government purchases, social security contributions, etc.
2. It manages the national debt, redeeming stocks when they fall due

for repayment, and issuing fresh loan stock to replace the old, or when the government decides to borrow more.

3. It controls the money supply, the amount of coins and bank notes in circulation, and the amount of lending by the commercial banks by controlling the latter's deposits with the Central Bank.
4. It operates foreign exchange controls.
5. It helps to stabilize the rate of exchange by buying foreign currency when the domestic currency is considered too highly priced and the reverse when the domestic currency's exchange rate is slipping.
6. It represents the government on international monetary organizations.
7. It is the banker's bank. All commercial banks have accounts there and use them to make payments to one another due through the clearing house system.
8. It is a lender of last resort to other banks in temporary need of funds.
9. It looks after the country's gold and foreign currency reserves.
10. It sees to the printing, issue and recall of bank notes, and the issue and recall of coins, as well as the storage of notes and coins surplus to requirements.
11. It offers financial advice to the government.

RESEARCH TASK

Ask your parents or a friend or neighbour these questions:

- How often do they receive electricity and telephone bills?
- How much do they usually have to pay in a year?
- How much does car tax and insurance cost them for a year?
- How much do car repairs usually cost them in a year?
- How much rent (or loan or mortgage repayment) do they pay on their house each year?
- How much are their rates?
- How much do they usually spend on food each week?
- How much do they think the average person in their street receives (in salary or benefits) in a year?

Use this information to make a budget for the Tony family for a week; put down everything they will spend or pay in the week, and how much they will have to set aside for electricity and telephone bills, etc. They must also set aside some money for new clothes, special events, etc.

OR

Visit banks or financial institutions and collect copies of documents used in payments. Mount them and display, with labels saying what they are used for.

SELF-REVISION QUESTIONS

1. What are the essential features of money?
2. What is inflation? If it is running at a high rate, how might this affect the usefulness of money?
3. List the principal services offered by the commercial banks that might be used by:
   (a) A small-business manager who is thinking of opening a shop.
   (b) An importer of cigars from Cuba.
   (c) A private citizen.
   (Note: you may find it necessary to list the same service under more than one heading.)
4. What are the advantages of running a bank current account? Are there any disadvantages?
5. Find out the various types of deposit and savings accounts offered by the banks in your area and the rate of interest offered on each. How do the banks' facilities compare with those available through the Post Office Savings Bank?
6. Say what is meant by the following terms:
   (a) Open cheque.
   (b) Dishonoured cheque.
   (c) Bankers order.
   (d) Deposit slip.
7. Describe the aims and importance of personal budgeting.
8. What is the difference between short-term and long-term capital? Do you think that the distinction between the two is important?
9. Imagine you were opening a shop but did not have enough money to rent premises, fit them out and buy stock. Where might you find the capital to do this?
10. What is meant by security for a loan? Why is it important?
11. What are the advantages of life assurance to the citizen?
12. Why do governments insist on motorists insuring against the

damage they may cause in an accident, while house insurance is not compulsory?

13. Explain, with examples, the difference between insurance and gambling.
14. What is meant by the following insurance terms:
    (a) Average.
    (b) Utmost good faith.
    (c) Sum assured (or insured).
    (d) Proposal.
    (e) Premium.
15. What are the services provided by a Central Bank that are useful to other banks?
16. Explain how a Central Bank controls the money supply. Why is this important?
17. If your country decided to abandon its existing currency and switch to US dollars, would it still need a Central Bank? Give reasons.

10

The role of government

Security of the state

The role of government is primarily to carry out the will of the people as expressed in Parliament by their elected representatives. This is effected by passing laws, which are enforced partly by the police and other government agencies bringing prosecutions before the criminal law courts, and partly by private citizens who have suffered wrong by the acts of others suing for damages in the civil courts. Two important points should be noted. First, compliance with the law is compulsory – penalties such as fines and imprisonment are laid down for those who break the law. Second, however, law enforcement is not arbitrary. The police decide whether you are prosecuted: they do not decide whether you are guilty, or what the punishment should be – that is the function of the courts, which operate independently and impartially.

Others are also involved in the security of the state – the armed forces which protect it from attack by enemy countries, the prison service and so on. The fire service plays an important part in protecting citizens' property from damage by fire.

The wider role of government

At one time it was thought that government should do no more than defend the country, the citizens and their property. This was the so-called *laissez faire* philosophy. It has few supporters today. A few moments' consideration of the many services which are essential to modern life – from sewerage to transport to education – will show why this theory is no longer popular. Even if these services are not provided directly by the government, close government regulation is essential if they are to function smoothly.

Governments have also taken increasing interest in the health and well-being of their citizens as individuals, through free or subsidized health services, free education, state pensions, sick pay, unemployment benefits, etc. These are together known as *social security*. The social security provisions vary from one Caribbean country to another. For the sake of simplicity, only those operating in Trinidad are described below. Readers in other countries should compare the Trinidadian system with those in their own country.

Social insurance

Social insurance is undertaken in Trinidad and Tobago through what is called National Insurance, which is run by a government-controlled board. Both the employer and the employee have to contribute each week by purchasing insurance stamps from the nearest National Insurance Office and sticking them on the employee's contribution card. (The employer buys the stamps but part of the cost – one-third – is deducted from the employee's wages.) To obtain social insurance benefits, the employee has to have made a minimum contribution, i.e. have a minimum number of stamps on his card. Contributions are on a sliding scale, varying according to the wages earned, but with a maximum employee's contribution of $28.50 per month.

The following are some of the occasions on which the government will pay social insurance:

1. Loss of earnings through illness.
2. Maternity benefit.
3. Widow's benefit – for life or until she remarries.
4. Disability benefit – the wife in this case has to be the 'breadwinner' and responsible for the well-being of her husband.
5. Child allowance – paid up to the age of 16 (or 19 if the child is receiving full-time education).
6. Orphan's allowance.
7. Dependent parent's pension – this will be paid if the dead worker was the person upon whom the parents depended.
8. Pension – paid on retirement of the worker.
9. Invalidity benefit – this differs from (1) above in that it is paid to those who have been ill for some time and are likely to be permanent invalids.

Social assistance

This is designed for those in need who would not qualify for social insurance benefits. There are two other differences:

1. Payments are made at the discretion of officers in the government's social assistance department, who may pay an on-the-spot visit to

determine whether the applicant is a fit person to be given public assistance. The applicant has no legal *right* to benefit.

2. Applicants do not have to contribute. The cost is borne by the tax-payers.

An old-age pension is usually given to people who have reached the age of 65 and whose income is very small. Other allowances are given on merit.

It should be noted that public assistance is not new. It dates back to the reign of Queen Elizabeth I in England. However, in the past it was often unsystematic and inadequate.

Economic responsibilities

In the twentieth century, governments have taken conscious steps to improve the general welfare of citizens, through promoting economic growth and industrial and agricultural development, full employment, retraining of workers in declining industries and improving the general standard of living, particularly of the poorer sections of the community. They have also been concerned to maintain the stability of the currency and a favourable balance of payments, as described in Chapter 12.

Government intervention in business

To improve the economic situation, and to help and protect citizens, governments often intervene in the operation of business. One very important aspect is that of consumer protection, described in Chapter 7. Other methods of control include:

1. *Price controls.* The government may pass laws limiting the price that can be charged for essential commodities, or for items which are in short supply. The motive is to ensure that items such as bread or rice can still be bought by poorer members of the community.
   Disadvantages are:
   (a) The controls are difficult to enforce.
   (b) Because profits are reduced to manufacturers or retailers, there is little incentive to produce the item, which may become in even shorter supply.
   (c) Goods tend to be driven onto the 'black market' – unofficial or illegal sales at uncontrolled prices.
2. *Trading standards.* Special departments are set up to control fair trading in all sections of the community. They check that:
   (a) All goods are properly labelled.

(b) Weights and measures are accurate.
(c) Food-selling establishments are clean (they may also require a licence).
(d) Goods are in saleable condition.

3. *Subsidies.* These are cash grants given by the governments of the Caribbean to entrepreneurs to encourage them to carry out worthwhile activities that might not otherwise be economic. They are mostly given to farmers to encourage them to grow certain crops. Agricultural officers, appointed by the Minister of Agriculture, deal with applications and check that the conditions for the grant have been carried out.

   Subsidies are also given to some importers of goods so that the goods can be sold at a cheaper price to the customer. The government does this so that the cost of living can be kept down. For instance, the government of Trinidad subsidizes the import of rice from Guyana.

   Just occasionally, subsidies may be given to a manufacturer or industry that is facing a difficult period. This is to stop the industry closing down and throwing employees out of work.
4. *Import controls* can help to protect local industries which could not stand up to foreign competition, by making the price of imported goods more expensive. They may also be used to cut down the total amount of imports, to prevent balance-of-payments difficulties.
5. *Taxation* (see below) can be used to encourage certain industries (by giving tax concessions), and discourage others, such as cigarette manufacture (by levying very high taxes).

Taxation

A tax is a compulsory payment to the government. Taxes are needed to pay for the running of government (civil servants' and MPs' salaries, etc.) and for the services which the government provides to the community, mostly free of charge, but sometimes at less than the true cost. As mentioned above, they can also be used as an instrument of social or economic policy – but most money raised by taxation is used to pay for essential services.

It is usually the job of the Finance Ministry to work out how much money will be needed to pay for government services in the coming year, and to put forward suggestions on which taxes should be used, and at which rate they should be levied. These proposals are put to Parliament in the annual Budget, and, if approved, passed into law in an annual Finance Act.

Ideally, all taxes should satisfy the following conditions:

1. They should be easy and cheap to collect, and it should be difficult for unscrupulous citizens to evade payment.
2. Their yield should be certain – i.e. it should be relatively easy for citizens to work out how much tax they should pay.
3. They should be fair in their incidence on different sections of the community; for instance, it is generally thought that poor people should pay less tax than the rich, because they have less money to spare after they have paid for basic necessities.
4. They should not discourage enterprise and damage the economic life of the nation.

In practice, no single tax is ideal. The government usually uses a variety of taxes, which, taken together, are acceptable to the electorate and spread the tax burden fairly over the community.

Taxes are usually divided into two classes – direct and indirect.

Direct taxes are so called because they are levied directly on the individual citizen, or on companies. The chief direct taxes are:

1. Income tax – by far the most important source of revenue to most governments.
2. Corporation tax – similar to income tax, but levied on companies rather than individuals.
3. Death duties – levied on the money left by a dead person.
4. Capital gains tax – levied on the increased value of assets.
5. Unemployment levy – a form of social security contribution.

The main advantage of direct taxes is that the rate charged can be varied to suit the circumstances of the taxpayer; for example, income tax is charged at progressively higher and higher rates on successive 'slices' of income, so that the rich pay a lot of income tax, the poor little or none. The disadvantages are that they are expensive to collect and administer; there are often disputes between citizens and tax officials on the amount of tax due; and some citizens forget to put enough by to pay their taxes. For this reason employees pay income tax under the 'pay as you earn' (PAYE) system – the tax is deducted by the employer before the wages are paid.

Indirect taxes are those levied on goods or services. They are so called because the average taxpayer only pays them indirectly; the tax is paid by the manufacturer or importer, who passes the cost on to the consumer indirectly in the form of higher prices. Examples of indirect taxes are:

1. Stamp duty – on cheques, receipts, etc.
2. Purchase tax – usually paid by the manufacturer when he sells goods to the retailer.

3. Import duty – also known as customs duty.
4. Excise duty – similar in effect to import duty, but levied on certain home-produced goods.
5. Rates and property taxes – usually raised by local government authorities.
6. Value Added Tax – a form of purchase or sales tax.

The advantages of indirect taxes are: they are easy and cheap to collect; they are difficult to evade; and there is usually no argument over the amount due (although where purchase tax is charged at different rates, there may be difficult 'borderline' cases). The disadvantage is that everyone, rich or poor, must pay in the end, at the same rate. Because of this, most governments are careful not to tax basic necessities of life. They also tend to increase the cost of living and may discourage trade if they make certain goods so expensive that people are no longer willing to buy them.

Government assistance to industry and commerce

All Caribbean governments give assistance to the industry and commerce of their country, though this assistance takes many forms and varies from one country to another. Most governments have set up special ministries to deal with industry and commerce, with specially qualified experts in the industrial, economic, financial and legal fields.

The following are some of the ways in which Caribbean governments help, though they will not all apply in any one territory:

1. Information about foreign markets and trading opportunities.
2. Special sections in embassies abroad advertising the country's products and fostering the country's overseas trade. They will also protest to foreign governments when trade is threatened by foreign countries' import controls or regulations.
3. Where necessary experts are 'imported' on secondment from other governments or universities to help develop a particular field. This, of course, only happens when there are no suitably qualified locals for the job.
4. Governments set aside large areas for industrial development, like the Point Lisas area in Trinidad.
5. New industrial areas are provided with essential services, such as concrete roads, water supply, drains and electricity.
6. Governments make grants to business people. Most governments have set up special corporations to consider requests for credit that the commercial banks are unwilling to meet; the Industrial

Development Corporation in Trinidad is a good example of a department designed to help the small-business manager.

7. New industries may be allowed a 'tax holiday' – a period when they pay reduced (or no) taxes while they 'get on their feet'.
8. New industries may be allowed to import machinery duty free.
9. The government may forbid the import of certain goods if they are being produced locally.
10. Alternatively (as described above) imported goods may be heavily taxed.
11. Insurance aid against bad debts overseas is being set up in some territories through an Export Credits Guarantee Department.
12. The government may build factories, etc. and then lease them out to industrialists and businessmen, who could not afford to build them themselves.
13. The government may nationalize an ailing industry, to prevent its closure.
14. The government may sponsor and/or pay for training courses for businessmen, skilled craftsmen and technicians at universities, technical colleges or vocational schools.
15. Governments have set up departments where all kinds of trade information can be obtained.
16. Foreign companies may be encouraged to set up local factories or assembly plants, or to invest in local industries. Such investment is usually carefully controlled so that a fair share of the wealth so created remains in the host country.

Finally, one should not forget the important help that governments give more indirectly, by providing an efficient education system to train the skilled and reliable manpower needed in the modern world to build roads, bridges, harbours and other transport facilities; to maintain post and telecommunication services; and to do what it can to protect industrial and commercial property from theft and damage by fire by maintaining police and fire services.

ACTIVITY

Find out what type of social security is provided by the government of your country. How do people contribute to this, and who contributes? Write a report on this.

SELF-REVISION QUESTIONS

1. Explain what is meant by the *laissez-faire* theory of government. Why is it generally thought unsatisfactory in the twentieth century?
2. What is social security? Give examples of its operation in your own country.
3. Discuss whether the existence of social security benefits is likely to result in people working harder or less hard.
4. How does social security differ from social assistance? Why is the latter necessary?
5. Define taxation.
6. Give three examples of both direct and indirect taxes in force in your country.
7. List ten items of government expenditure that need to be financed by taxation.
8. It is sometimes said that direct taxes tend to benefit the poor, while indirect taxes tend to benefit the rich. Why should this be so?
9. Explain the difference between customs and excise duty.
10. In an imaginary country, income tax is levied as follows. The first $2,000 per year is free of income tax. In addition, citizens receive further tax-free allowance of $1,000 p.a. for a wife and $750 p.a. for each child under 16. All remaining income is taxed at the following rates:

1st	$2,000	10%
Next	$5,000	30%
Next	$2,000	35%
Next	$2,000	40%
Thereafter		50%

    Calculate the yearly tax bill for:
    (a) A single man earning $5,000 a year.
    (b) A married man with three children (all under 16) and earning $5,500 a year.
    (c) A married man with no children earning $15,000 a year.
    (d) An unmarried woman earning $500 per month.
11. In the same country, import duty on cars is 10% of the import price, including freight. In addition, there is 20% purchase tax on the price after duty. Calculate the total cost of a car purchased in the UK for $8,000 plus $400 freight and insurance.

12. What are the advantages and disadvantages of price controls? Do you know of any commodity which has its price controlled in your country?
13. List *three* reasons for charging import duty.
14. What are the four desirable features of taxation? To what extent do (a) income tax; and (b) purchase tax meet these criteria?
15. Find out what assistance is available to industry in your country, and, where possible, the responsible government department in each case.

11

Elements of economics

Determining the selling price

Fixing the correct price at which to sell one's goods is one of the most important and difficult marketing decisions. The price people are prepared to pay for an item usually depends on *supply* and *demand.* If demand increases (because more people want to buy, perhaps because they have more money), prices tend to rise; this has occurred with fruit and vegetables in Trinidad. This may encourage more people to produce the item, until supply and demand are in balance again, and the price stops rising. Likewise, if an item (like coconuts) is in short supply because of disease or crop failure, prices will again go up.

On the other hand, if fewer people want to buy, perhaps because the item is going out of fashion, or because there is a lot of unemployment, then prices tend to fall, because producers and shopkeepers will try reducing prices to tempt people to buy. Also, if there is a surplus or *glut,* perhaps because there has been a very heavy crop, prices will again fall as producers tempt people to buy more than usual.

This process is illustrated in the diagram (Figure 11.1). Between points C and D on the curve, demand is said to be *elastic,* that is to say, as the price goes up, the quantity bought goes down more or less in proportion. When, however, the price rises above \$A, nearly everyone thinks it is too expensive and demand falls off very quickly indeed. Conversely, as the price is reduced, so the quantity bought goes up till it reaches B units. There is, however, a limit to the quantity which people want or need of any commodity, however cheap it may be, and further price reductions below \$E have little or no effect in increasing sales. This process is easy enough to understand. The difficulty in practice lies in giving cash or quantity figures which correspond with the various points on the diagram. The values will not only vary from one commodity to another, but also from month to month as people's attitudes and the amount of money they have to spend will also vary.

Naturally there are exceptions to this general pattern. Demand for some goods is relatively *inelastic,* that is, relatively unaffected by change in price.

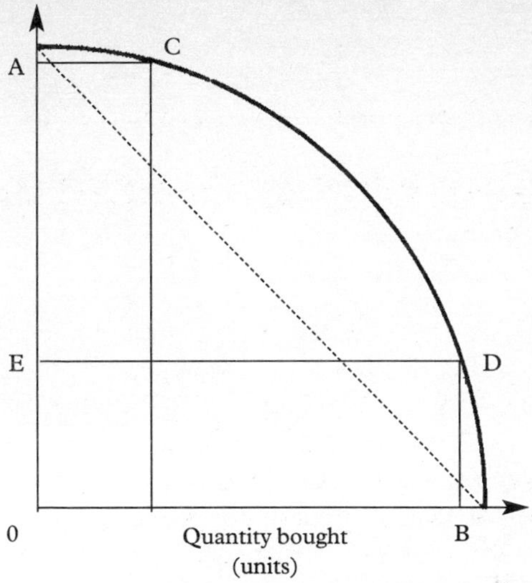

Figure 11.1 Normal supply and demand curve

This often applies to essential foodstuffs. For instance, everyone must eat some salt for good health, but they only need a certain quantity and reducing the price will not induce them to eat more. Elasticity of demand is also affected by the availability of substitutes. Imagine for instance, an island where the only energy-giving foods available are bananas and plantains. If the price of plantains went up, people would continue to buy their normal quantity, or go hungry. In normal circumstances, however, if the price of plantains rose too high, people would stop buying them and switch to other foods such as rice, sweet potato, cocoyams, etc.

A manufacturer or shopkeeper will incur *costs* in making, obtaining and selling his goods. If his sales income is higher than his cost, he makes a *profit*. If his costs are higher than his income, he makes a loss. Any business that makes a loss for more than a short period must cease trading or risk bankruptcy. Businesspeople therefore always try to deal only in goods and services which they can provide at a profit.

Costs can be classified in various ways. One way is to divide them into *direct* and *indirect* costs.

1. *Direct costs* are those which vary directly with the level of production. For a manufacturer, they would be: raw materials, wages of workers directly employed on making the product, and other directly attributable costs such as electricity to run machinery and transport costs. For a shopkeeper, direct cost will be the purchase price of the goods he sells, plus carriage.

2. *Indirect costs or overheads* are those which do not vary directly with production levels. They will include such things as rent, rates, lighting, staff wages, selling expenses, stationery and advertising.

It is a simple matter to calculate direct costs. They are simply added together. To calculate direct costs per unit, the total is divided by the number of units produced. Indirect costs are more difficult to calculate, but they must be included if the business manager is to be sure that the price covers all the costs and leaves a profit; some inexperienced traders get into financial difficulties because they forget about or underestimate their indirect costs. The most usual method is *overhead absorption*. The business manager looks at the past year's accounts and calculates the total amount of the overheads. He or she then compares this with the total amount of the direct costs and adds the same proportion to the direct cost of each product in order to make sure of covering costs or *breaking even*. An example may make this clearer.

A. TRADER

Trading and Profit and Loss Account for year ended 31 Dec. 1998

		$		$
Opening stock		6,000	Sales	40,000
Add Purchases		28,000		
		34,000		
Less Closing stock		4,000		
Cost of goods sold (direct costs)		30,000		
Gross profit	*C/d*	*10,000*		
		40,000		*40,000*
Transport		1,000	Gross profit bid	10,000
Insurance		2,000		
Rent and rates		500		
Total indirect costs		3,500		
Net profit		6,500		
		$10,000		$10,000

Indirect costs as % of direct costs – $3,500 – 0.1167 = 11.7% $30,000

Net profit as % of direct costs = $6,500 – 0.2167 = 21.7%
$30,000

To cover the indirect costs A. Trader must add a minimum of 11.7% to the cost of each item she buys. To make the same level of profit as in 1998, she must add a further 21.7% (total 33.3%). This is known as her mark-up. This means that an article she buys for $10 will be marked up to at least $13.33 in her shop. She may, of course, charge more than this if she thinks customers are prepared to pay more. This depends on how badly they want the article, and on what other shops are charging.

What if she cannot sell the article for $13.33? If it is an isolated item, she will reduce the price, or put it in a sale, to get what cash she can for it, and make a note not to stock this item again. If however it is her main line of business, she has a more difficult choice. She can reduce the price as low as $11.17 and still cover her costs (purchase price $10 + overhead absorption $1.17). Below $11.17 she will incur a net loss, but it may still be worth her while to go on trading in the item, at least in the short term, because every cent she can charge over $10 will at least be making a *contribution* to covering her overheads. It could well be that if she simply ceased selling the item, her sales might be halved (to $20,000 p.a.) but her overheads would still remain much the same. She would then have to increase the mark-up on her remaining goods to $15,000 or 23.3% to break even, and to 66.7% to maintain her previous level of cash profit. This might be impossible without driving customers away from her store completely.

(*Note:* accountants may prefer to calculate profit as a percentage of selling price. In the above accounts, the gross profit is $\frac{\$10{,}000}{£40{,}000} = 25\%$

and the net profit $\underline{\$6{,}500} = 16.25\%$.)

The manufacturer must also distinguish between *fixed* and *variable costs.* Some costs, such as those of operating and depreciating machinery and equipment, will remain fixed however many units are produced, while others, such as the cost of raw materials, will vary directly according to the number of units made. Clearly, he must sell a certain number of units before he will cover his costs, as Figure 11.2 shows.

If, however, goods are produced to order in a large batch by an outside supplier, then *all* costs are fixed, as Figure 11.3 indicates. It is important to note that in this case the calculated profit will only be made if all the goods in the batch are sold.

Value and price

Value can be said to be the power of goods or service to attract other goods or services in exchange for itself. Price on the other hand is the market value of the goods or service in terms of money.

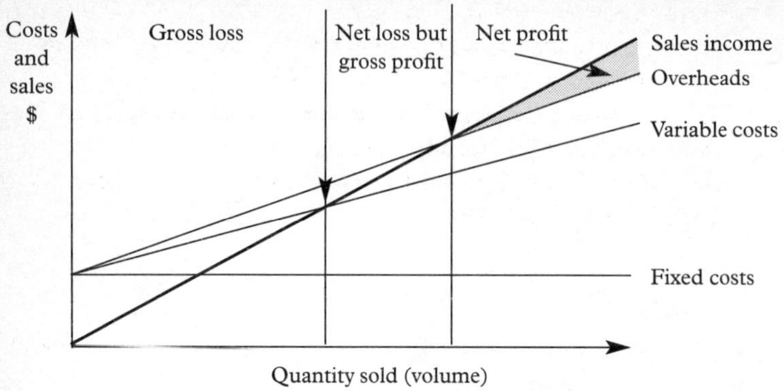

Figure 11.2 Break-even (or profit/volume) chart

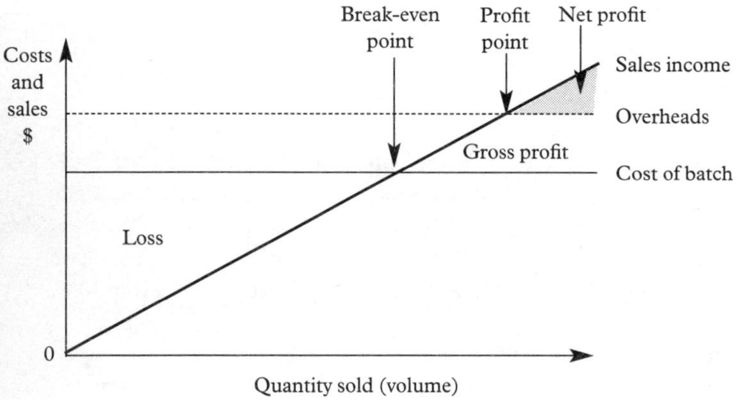

Figure 11.3 Break-even chart (batch production)

The price system

In any competitive economy prices are left to be determined by the forces of demand and supply.

Advantages of the price system

1. Prices indicate market forces.
2. Output and expenditure can be controlled.
3. Helps to control the balance between demand and supply.
4. Helps to ration goods that are scarce so people who can afford to pay for them may buy them, provided there are less expensive alternatives for others to buy.
5. Allocation of resources becomes more effective.
6. People have freedom of choice and freedom of enterprise.

Disadvantages of the price system

1. It is disadvantageous to the low-income consumer, as many essential things may be beyond their means to pay.
2. The fluctuation of prices may create uncertainty among buyers and sellers, and this affects future planning.
3. Demand may be influenced by advertising or fashion, rather than the real needs of people.

Price control

The government of your country may control prices for the following reasons:

1. To protect buyers in general.
2. To protect the poorer community.

Equilibrium price

This is the price at which demand is equal to supply. In Figure 11.4 OY is the price axis, and OX shows the quantity demanded and supplied.

DD is a demand curve – as the price goes down, demand rises.

SS is a supply curve; the higher the price, the more suppliers want to supply.

The point M shows the price at which demand is equal to supply. M represents market.

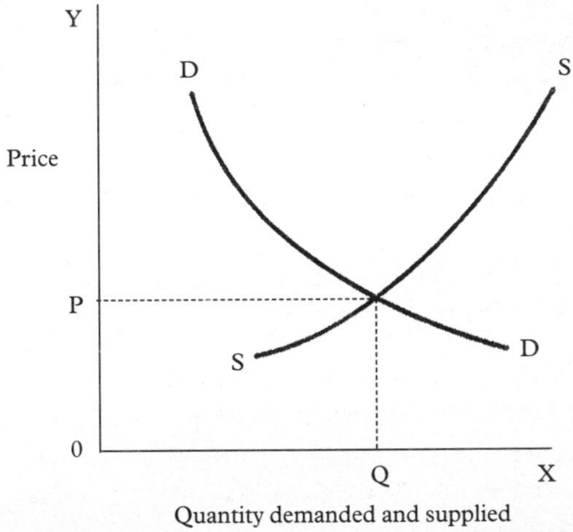

Figure 11.4 Supply and demand curve in relation to equilibrium price

Demand and supply

In the study of economics you must not look at demand as meaning want, desire or need. You will have to look at the amount a consumer is willing to demand at a given price per unit of time. For example, you can say that there is a demand for 10,000 school shirts at $25 each. This is what economics calls effective demand.

Factors affecting the demand of individuals

The following factors determine how much of a unit will be demanded by an individual at a particular price at a particular time:

1. The price of goods/services.
2. The utility that could be derived from the goods/services.
3. The availability of substitutes.
4. The selling price of substitutes.
5. The quality of substitutes.
6. The income of the consumer.
7. The tastes and habits of the consumer.
8. The standard of living of the consumer.
9. Government intervention.

Supply

As with demand, you have to look at supply as the amount of goods or services actually offered for sale at a particular price per unit of time (opposite of demand). 10,000 shirts can be supplied at $25 each.

Factors affecting supply

The following factors will determine how much of a unit could be supplied by a firm at a particular price at a particular time:

1. Market price fluctuation of the item to be sold.
2. Changes in the techniques of production.
3. Cost of labour.
4. Other costs of production.
5. Government policy, e.g. tax rises.
6. Intensity of competition.
7. Cost of distribution.

Elasticity of supply

This is the responsiveness of supply to any change that may occur to price. Whenever a small variation in price causes a very big change in supply, supply is said to be elastic.

Monopolies and cartels

A *monopoly* exists where there is only one seller or provider of a product or service. Strictly speaking, where there are only two producers, there is *duopoly* and where there are more than two, but still only a few, there is *oligopoly*. However, in practice the word monopoly is used to cover *all* these situations. There are several different types of monopoly:

1. *De facto* or *commercial monopoly*. This occurs when one company has 'cornered the market' by take-overs, amalgamations or squeezing out all competitors. It is generally regarded as undesirable, because the consumer has no choice and there is no competition.
2. *Statutory monopoly*, for instance, one water company, one electricity supplier, one telephone company. As explained in Chapter 2, it would be absurd to have more than one provider of these utilities. They are called statutory, because the monopoly is established by Act of Parliament (statute). They may be publicly or privately owned.
3. *Legal monopoly*. The inventor of a new process or device can *patent* it. He or she registers details with the government patent office, and no one else is allowed to copy it for a given period of years.
4. *Natural monopoly*. Some country may have a monopoly of supply of a certain raw material, because it is found nowhere else. For instance, South Africa and Russia have a virtual monopoly on the world's gold supply.

The advantage of monopoly is that, if production is in the hands of only one organization, it can profit from the economies of scale. The disadvantages are:

1. There is restriction of choice.
2. There is no competition on price or service, often leading to a 'Take it or leave it' attitude.
3. Supply is often artificially restricted, again pushing up prices.
4. There is no incentive to efficiency or improvement.

For these reasons, most governments now take steps to prevent commercial monopolies developing. Where they are unavoidable, they are usually strictly controlled and the prices they charge may be subject to government approval.

A special type of monopoly is the sole distributorship, where one firm has the exclusive right to import and sell a foreign company's products. This is quite common in the Caribbean. Many foreign motor manufacturers operate this system. There is, of course, stiff competition from similar products from other manufacturers.

Monopsony occurs when there is only one buyer. In most Caribbean territories, the telephone company is the only buyer for telephone equipment, the electricity supply undertaking the only buyer for large electric generators, and so on.

A *cartel* (also known as a *ring* or *corner)* occurs when a group of companies agree to regulate the market by restricting supply, charging the same prices and avoiding direct competition with each other. This is only effective if between them they control a substantial part of the market. The effects are the same as those of monopoly. Cartels have been made illegal in many countries. On an international scale they are more difficult for individual governments to control. Two well-known examples of international cartels are the conference system, where shipping lines sailing between the same ports agree to charge the same rates, and the Organization of Petroleum Exporting Countries (OPEC), which fixes the price of crude oil.

Perfect market

In economics, the word 'market' means the general conditions in which buying and selling take place.

A perfect market is the opposite of a perfect monopoly, but in real life most markets are somewhere in between.

Characteristics of a perfect market and perfect competition

1. Entry to the market must be free.
2. There must be a large number of buyers and sellers who must compete freely among themselves; otherwise a large buyer/seller may be powerful enough to influence the price.
3. Dealing among the buyers and sellers should be carried out in any part of the market.
4. The goods or services being dealt with must be homogeneous and standardized, so that the only difference between different sellers is one of price.
5. The buyers and sellers must have full knowledge of conditions of demand, supply and price.
6. No one should be given preferential treatment.
7. All actions between buyers and sellers must be based on price only – nothing else.
8. There must be no trade restriction.
9. All must be able to communicate freely.

Market imperfection and imperfect competition

From what you have just read you will realize that a perfect market cannot be achieved and so all markets are to be considered imperfect. The following conditions may make a market imperfect:

1. Many sources of supply are monopolistic, so that even though there may be many sellers, there is only one source of supply, which can control the price.
2. Many buyers are monopolists. They may join together to get lower prices.
3. Many buyers and sellers lack information on market conditions.
4. There is government intervention in markets.
5. Many trade practices are restrictive in nature; this means that the price to a certain buyer may be affected by other factors which are nothing to do with this particular sale.
6. Products may not be homogeneous and so cannot be compared exactly with each other, for example there are different brands of tea, with different tastes.

ACTIVITY

Choose two products which people in your age-group buy, e.g. CDs and shirts: do a survey of ten people asking them what they would do if the price of the CD or school shirt they wanted were to double. Would they:

1. Not buy it and go without.
2. Buy a different CD or a different brand of shirt which is cheaper (if there is one).
3. Still buy it anyway.

Do you get a different answer for the shirt from the answer for the CD? Why? Is demand for a CD more elastic, or inelastic than demand for a school shirt?

Display your findings in a chart.

SELF-REVISION QUESTIONS

1. Explain the difference between elastic and inelastic demand.
2. Under which conditions is an article likely to be *reduced* in price?

3. Explain why a distinction is made between direct and indirect costs when calculating profit.
4. What is the difference between gross profit and mark-up? If an article costs $4 and is sold for $5, what is (a) gross profit per cent; (b) the percentage mark-up?
5. What factors should a shopkeeper consider when deciding whether or not to stock an item in his shop?
6. What are the advantages and disadvantages of monopoly: (a) to the manufacturer; (b) to the consumer?
7. Discuss whether it would be a good thing if the Post Office ceased to have monopoly on carrying letters.
8. What is a cartel? Give an example.
9. What are the functions of a chamber of commerce?
10. Name a well-known trade association in your country and find out as much as you can about its work.
11. What is the difference between instalment selling and hire purchase?
12. Should hire purchase be encouraged or discouraged? Give reasons.
13. Study the price tag for a television set in Figure 11.5 and calculate:
    (a) The price to be paid for it if bought for spot cash (i.e. immediate payment).
    (b) The total hire purchase price. (Do not forget the deposit!)
    (c) The approximate rate of interest charged.

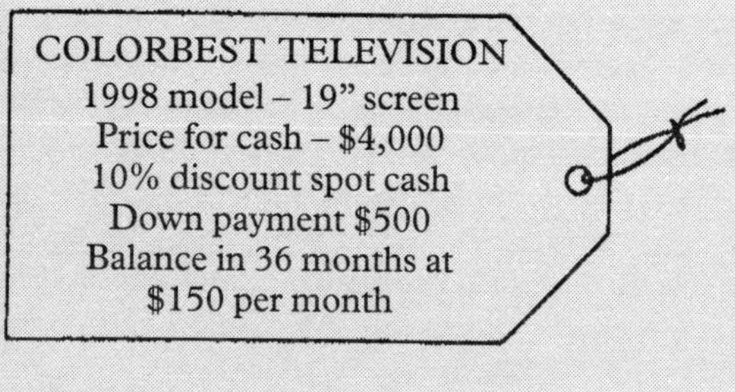

Figure 11.5 A hire purchase tag

14. K. Narayan buys goods to the value of $240 retail, but is allowed 25% trade discount on the invoice, plus 2% cash discount. How much does he have to pay?

15. State the circumstances under which a trader is likely to allow a discount to his customers.
16. Why is consumer protection legislation necessary?
17. Try to discover what protection is offered to the consumer in your country, by the law and government departments. Do you think this protection should be increased or reduced, or left as it is?
18. Explain the function of wholesalers. Do they contribute to increased prices to the consumer?
19. List the main types of retail outlet. Which is the most important in your country?
20. What are the advantages and disadvantages of a tied outlet?
21. Why is transport important?
22. What means of transport would be best for the following?
    (a) A cargo of bananas from Dominica to London.
    (b) Cement from Port of Spain to Tunapuna, Trinidad.
    (c) Cement from Port of Spain to Scarborough, Tobago.
    (d) Newspapers from New York to Montego Bay, Jamaica.
    (e) Newspapers from Kingston to Montego Bay.
23. List the ports and airports in your country.

12

Social accounting and international trade

Measuring the cost of living

The cost of living is measured in terms of how much can he bought with a person's income, usually after any income tax has been deducted. It is a strictly financial calculation. It does not take into account those aspects of the quality of life, such as the view from his or her house or how many friends he or she has, which cannot be measured in money terms.

In practice an average value has to be taken, covering the community as a whole, or large, easily identified sections of it (such as managers, agricultural workers, pensioners, etc.). It includes payments for 'intangibles' such as mortgages, rent and insurance and for 'unnecessary' items such as drink, entertainment and tobacco, as well as basic necessities such as food and clothing. Clearly, problems are involved in choosing which items to include in the calculation, as different people spend their income on different things. In practice, those items which are most frequently bought are generally used.

In measuring the cost of living of a community, the buying power of the dollar is of the utmost importance, because it is always changing. To take out this fluctuation in the value of the dollar and to determine real changes in income, a *price index* is constructed. The two most important indices are:

1. *The consumer price index.* This is popularly known as the cost-of-living index. It is made up of the prices of goods and services purchased by the consumer. It plays an important role in the economy of Caribbean islands, since it is often used as the basis of wage negotiations. Wage rises linked to the cost of living would ensure that a worker's wages remained constant in 'real' terms.
2. *The index of wholesale prices.* This is an index of the cost of goods and services purchased by manufacturers and business people.

Both indices are constructed in the same way.

How to construct a cost-of-living index

Let us hire a man to follow the Roopnarine family for a year. Every time they buy something, they buy the same type and size of product. At the end of the year they have bought 52 packets of razor blades, 6 haircuts, 100 taxi rides, 365 loaves of bread, 700 bottles of milk and 12 dozen eggs. Let us say that the cost of all these things comes to $600. Since the Roopnarine is an average family we can then say that the cost of living of the average family is $600. This was in 1997. We call this the base year. In the succeeding year, we take the same goods and the same services and we reprice them. In 1998, the total cost of these goods and services was $800. We say that the index figure in the base year was 100. To get the index figure for 1998, we divide $800 by $600 and multiply by 100, giving a result of 133.3. In other words, what you could have bought for $100 in 1997 would have cost you, on average, $133.33 in 1998; or the cost of living has gone up by 33.3%.

Meanwhile, Mr Roopnarine has negotiated a *25%* wage increase with his employer. He is delighted, until our man tells him that his standard of living has actually gone down by:

$$100 - \frac{125}{1.333} = 100 - \frac{1500}{16} = 100 - 93.75 = 6\tfrac{1}{4}\%$$

Gross national product

Gross domestic product (GDP) is the total value of all the goods and all the services produced in a country during a particular year. This concept is easy to understand, but measurement presents certain difficulties. First, does 'value' mean cost of production, wholesale price or retail price? Cost of production is usually chosen, and this is often known as *factor cost.* Second, precautions must be taken against double counting. For instance, suppose a farmer sells some sugar cane to a refinery for $100. This is then refined and the sugar sold in bulk to a wholesaler for $150, who then bags it for sale to retailers. The full $150 must not be added to the original $100, but only the added value of $50. Third, some wealth, particularly agricultural products consumed on the farm where they were grown, never enters into commerce at all. An estimate has to be made of the value of such production.

To determine *gross national product* (GNP), the GDP figure must be adjusted by deducting profits, wages, etc. remitted abroad and adding profits, wages, etc. earned abroad and remitted home. The result, also know as *national income,* is the money value of the flow of goods and services which becomes available to a nation during a year for consumption or for adding to its wealth.

In addition to calculating the gross domestic product by adding up national income, it is also possible to obtain it by adding up the total *national expenditure,* since what is earned is at the same time spent by someone else. It is necessary, of course, to make appropriate allowances for savings.

If a country is prosperous, its national income will increase faster than that of its poorer neighbours. The following are some of the factors that determine the national income of a country:

1. The political stability of the country.
2. The state of development of its industry and commerce.
3. The size and quality of its labour force.
4. Its natural resources and how easy they are to exploit.
5. Its existing capital resources.
6. The entrepreneurial skill deployed.

Finally, the warning needs to be repeated that changes in the value of money make comparison of the true significance of increases in GNP very difficult – not only comparing one year with another, but one country with another.

Income distribution

This measures how evenly the wealth of a country (measured by its GNP) is spread among the population. Even in communist countries distribution is never completely equal. Typically, there are a small number of very rich people, a larger number of moderately well-off people, and a very large number of people with comparatively low incomes. (There will also be some people who are destitute – with little or no income.) This is illustrated in the income distribution of an imaginary country shown in Figure 12.1.

In the nineteenth century, wealth tended to be concentrated in the hands of a few very wealthy planters and landowners. There was a comparatively small middle class of merchants, doctors, clergymen, etc. The majority of the population earned very low wages. In the twentieth century, the number of really rich people reduced, but the middle class grew enormously and on the whole the working class were much better off. However, in some countries, gross inequalities of wealth still persist.

As explained in Chapter 10, the rich tend to pay more income tax than the poor. The very poor will pay little or no tax, since governments try to avoid taxing basic necessities. Much of the money collected may be used to pay pensions, family allowances, sickness benefit and other social security provisions. Thus there is a flow of money from citizens to

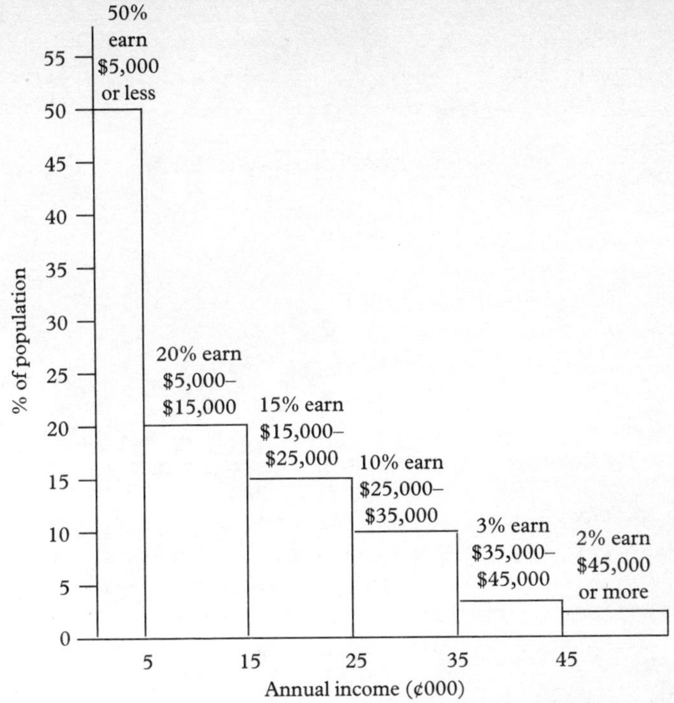

Figure 12.1 Typical pattern of income distribution

government, and from government to citizens, but the rich will pay more than they receive in benefits, while the less well-off will receive more than they pay. This process is known as *income redistribution.*

In Great Britain, the USA and other large countries, figures on income distribution are published by the government. They are of great value in estimating tax yields, the likely market for different types of product and the effect on individuals and families of government policies. Unfortunately, this information is not available in many Caribbean countries.

Savings and investment

Savings are the difference between income and the amount spent on current needs for a particular period of time. If income is greater than expenditure, savings will accumulate; if the reverse, accumulated savings will be reduced. For the business manager, profits are the main source of savings – the difference between revenue and expenditure.

Investment is business expenditure that results in two things: the purchase of a permanent asset, and, if all goes well, the production of income. The business person will invest in plant, machinery, premises and stock in the expectation of making a profit, while the private individual will invest in government securities, stocks and shares, in the expectation of receiving interest or dividends.

It is obvious that there cannot be investment without savings, but the amount of investment in a given period is not necessarily equivalent to the amount of savings made. Not all money saved is available for investment: everyone needs ready cash; shopkeepers need money for change; banks need till money to finance demands from their customers. Sometimes, however, investment can be greater than savings. It is possible, though unlikely, for a government to finance investment from taxation. Banks can increase the amount of money in circulation by *credit creation,* as is shown in the following example.

Suppose someone puts $1,000 of savings in a bank. The bank's main source of income is the interest on loans, and it knows that at any one time it will only be called upon to repay a small proportion of the money lent to it. Thus it may place, say, 15% in reserve and lend the other $850 to a customer. This enables the customer to pay a bill for $850 for supplies, and the supplier, having no immediate need for the money, puts it on deposit in the bank. Bank B keeps 10% in reserve and lends $765 to another customer. And so on. Even if the process were continued no further, already $1,000 has created $850 + 765 = $1,615 of credit. In practice, the process is likely to be less rapid, but as more money chasing the same quantity of goods is one way of causing inflation, it is obvious why governments sometimes resort to a 'credit squeeze'.

Growth and development

Economic growth means a real increase in the GNP of a nation, after the effects of inflation have been taken into account. This will only result in an improved standard of living, however, if the rate of growth is higher than the rate of increase in the population. As population is increasing as a result of improved medical care nearly everywhere in the world, it is clear why governments place such importance on growth when working out their economic policies.

Development in economics means providing the wherewithal to exploit natural resources to maximum advantage – it covers everything from government organizations, educational facilities and financial institutions (providing credit and finance), to transport, storage, processing and telecommunication facilities. A highly developed country will be in a better position to exploit its natural resources than an underdeveloped one and will probably enjoy a higher standard of living. Most developed countries are to be found in Europe and North America, to which Japan, Australia and South Africa must be added. Most under-developed countries are to be found in Africa and Asia. The Caribbean countries and the states of Central and South America are in an intermediate category. Everywhere, however, there are significant differences between nearby countries which are not always easy to explain: in Europe, Switzerland and Germany are highly developed, Albania and Bulgaria still very backward.

Development must not be confused with size. Brazil, with over 100 million inhabitants, is at roughly the same stage of development as Trinidad, a very small country. Nor should development be confused with wealth. In 1976 the average income per head was US$13,250 in Kuwait and in the United Kingdom $3,870. The UK is much more highly developed, but Kuwait has large oil revenues and a very small population. On the whole, however, under-developed countries are poor – compare these figures with $224 for Kenya and $135 for Tanzania.

The following features are characteristic of under-developed and developing countries:

1. Low standards of living.
2. Slow rate of growth of income – caused either by poor economic performance or by the population exceeding growth.
3. Shorter life expectancy – because of poor food and medical care.
4. Poor educational opportunities.
5. High rates of population growth.
6. High levels of unemployment.
7. A large proportion of the population engaged in agriculture.

Governments of these countries face immense problems in trying to improve their economies. Some of these problems are:

1. Rapid increase in the population. One of the first effects of improved medical care is that more children and old people survive. This makes the problems of feeding and providing work for the population even more difficult.
2. Difficulties in increasing agricultural production. An increasing population needs more land for housing, schools, etc. Modern farming techniques may not be suitable for the tropics or on very small farms.
3. A lack of capital for investment in roads, factories, etc. If this money is borrowed from abroad, high rates of interest may have to be paid. Many developing countries have great difficulty in meeting the interest payments on their loans, let alone getting around to paying the money back.

4. Difficulties in adapting foreign technology. This is often:
   (a) Capital-intensive, i.e. very expensive.
   (b) Labour-saving, thus often reducing employment opportunities.
   (c) Very complicated and sophisticated, needing highly skilled engineers to look after it.
5. Development plans are sometimes over-ambitious.
6. Data needed for reliable planning may not be available – possibly leading to expensive mistakes.
7. Unanticipated economic factors, which may deprive the government of income it had been relying on to put its development plans into effect. This is particularly likely if a country relies almost exclusively for its foreign earnings on one basic commodity, such as bauxite (Jamaica) or sugar, whose price may suddenly drop. The rapid increase in oil prices has also been a severe problem for many developing countries.
8. Lack of organization at government level. Civil servants in many developing countries are very badly trained and inefficient.
9. Lack of co-operation from key sections of the population. This is very likely if there is political unrest.

It is clearly essential for all citizens to work together for the common good to overcome or prevent these problems.

The importance of international trade

If goods or services can be produced more cheaply abroad, then there is an obvious advantage in importing them, rather than producing them locally. World-wide, this leads to lower costs of production and therefore a higher standard of living. However, there are often short-term advantages to a national government, in protecting employment and the value of its currency, in restricting imports, by outright prohibition, quotas or high import duties. This has an adverse effect on international trade, because one country's imports are another country's exports.

It is one of the aims of international co-operation therefore to get countries to lower or abolish import duties. The organizations and agreements which achieve this are described in Chapter 13.

Balance of trade and balance of payments

The *balance of* trade is the difference between the value of a country's visible exports and its imports. These are usually measured monthly and summarized every year. If a country exports more than it imports, it has a favourable balance of trade; if it imports more than it exports, it has an unfavourable balance of trade (a deficit).

The items entering into trade are divided into visible and invisibles. *Visibles* are actually goods, so called because they can be seen. *Invisibles* are payments for services and other intangible items. Invisible imports would include:

1. Money spent by business people and holidaymakers travelling abroad.
2. Insurance premiums paid to foreign insurance companies.
3. Interest payments on foreign loans.
4. Payments for goods and passengers carried on foreign-owned ships and aircraft.

Invisible exports include:

1. Tourist income – very important for many Caribbean islands.
2. Interest paid by foreigners on loans from domestic companies and citizens.
3. Receipts from foreigners for carrying goods and passengers on the country's own ships and aircraft.

Because of tourist income, many Caribbean countries make up their deficit on visible trade from invisible earnings.

The *balance of payments* is the balance of trade adjusted for net capital movements – public and private investment, wages sent home by those working abroad, development grants and loans and so on.

The following is the balance of payments of three imaginary countries for a year:

	A	B	C
	$m	$m.	$m
Exports	2,410	1,396	3,005
Imports	3,720	1,880	2,258
Balance of trade	–1,310	–484	+ 747
Invisible exports	2,335	314	1,176
Invisible imports	1,508	682	950
Balance of payments	+ 827	–368	+ 226
Balance of trade	–483	–852	+ 973
Net capital movements			
in (+) or out (–)	+ 647	–114	+ 863
Balance of payments	+ 164	–966	+1,836

A deficit on balance of payments must be financed by government loans from overseas banks or the International Monetary Fund (available in emergency only and subject to strict conditions), or by drawing on reserves of gold and foreign currencies. A surplus on the balance of payments is used to repay loans or build up reserves.

Clearly a country cannot continue for long to have an adverse balance of payments without getting into serious difficulties. The government must take some or all of the following steps to rectify the situation:

1. Impose a credit squeeze. This discourages borrowing and investment and tends to reduce the amount spent on imports. In the long term it is harmful, because it reduces growth and development.
2. Impose import restrictions or currency controls and increase import duties. This may increase the cost of living.
3. Devalue the currency. The effect of this can be shown as follows:

(1)	(2)
\$1 = 50p sterling	\$1 devalued to 30p sterling.
Home-produced item costs \$1.	Home-produced item costs \$1.
Imported item costs 40p.	Imported item costs 40p.
$40p = \frac{\$40}{50} = \$0.80$	$40p = \frac{\$40}{30} = \$1.33$
Imported item preferred.	Home-produced item now preferred
Drain on balance of payments.	Foreign exchange saved.

Devaluation also has disadvantages. Imported raw materials and essential foodstuffs will go up in price (in the above example by 33.3%), thus encouraging inflation. 33.3% more goods will have to be exported to earn the same amount of foreign currency.

ACTIVITY

Form a business club at your school. Collect together as much money as you can from teachers and students, and decide together on two different investments to put it in. Watch over the weeks how the value of these two stocks goes up or down. If you cannot collect money and make a real investment, you can do just the same thing with imaginary money. Each member of the class can have \$1,000 and choose an investment. Companies are listed in the newspaper and in the telephone book; they are usually happy to provide information about their activities. Each student may keep an individual record of how his or her investment gains in value, or this could be kept on a wall chart so that the different stocks can be compared.

If your country does not have a stock exchange you may be able to read about the stocks and shares on the Jamaica or Trinidad stock exchanges in your newspaper, and do the same activity.

SELF-REVISION QUESTIONS

1. How is the standard of living of one country compared with that of another?
2. Explain the difference between the retail and wholesale price indices. Which is normally used to measure the cost of living?
3. Discuss the factors which may lead to inflation.
4. Calculate the retail price index for 1998 and 1999 from the following information:

			Prices	
Commodity	*Qty used*	1990 (=100)	1998	1999
Bread	100 loaves	80¢ loaf	85¢	90¢
Fish	20 kg	$1.90kg	$1.85	$1.95
Vegetables	40kg	$1.20kg	$1.25	$1.45
Meat	10kg	$5.50kg	$5.25	$6.00

5. What is gross domestic product? What are the difficulties in its calculation?
6. Which of these is the 'odd man out'? Explain.
   National income.
   National expenditure.
   Gross domestic product.
   Gross national product.
7. Explain what is meant by income redistribution. What are the principal means by which it is achieved in your country?
8. Discuss whether you would expect greater or lesser inequalities of income distribution between: developed and under-developed countries; planned economies and mixed economies; 1960 and 1980 (in your own country).
9. Why do governments encourage savings?
10. What is meant by economic growth? How is it achieved?
11. Many countries achieved lower economic growth in the 1990s than in the 1970s and 1980s. What factors do you think were responsible?

12. List the obstacles to economic growth and development faced by the poorer countries in the world today.
13. What distinguishes a developed from an under-developed country?
14. If a country is faced with the alternative of negotiating a large loan or obtaining more favourable treatment from countries importing its staple export crop, which do you think it should choose?
15. Explain the difference between balance of payments and balance of trade.
16. What are invisible earnings? Give an example of importance to your country.
17. How is a deficit on the balance of payments financed?
18. Study the table of balance of payments on p.151:
    (a) Which country appears the most prosperous?
    (b) What might be one of the country A's major sources of foreign exchange? (Compare the figures for visible and invisible exports.)
    (c) Country A has a favourable balance of payments. Do you think this reflects a fundamentally sound economy?
19. Compare the merits of devaluation and import controls as means of correcting an unfavourable balance of payments.

13

The regional and international business environment

Caribbean economic institutions

Many countries in the Caribbean are small, and often poor. It is therefore necessary for them to work together for the common good (see Figure 13.1). By co-operation on an international scale, many things are

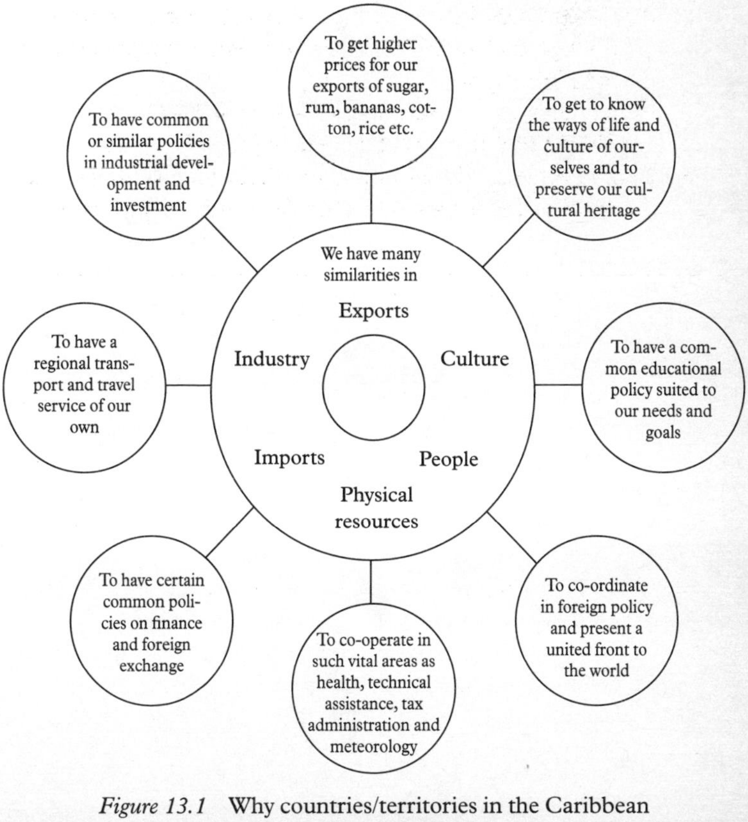

Figure 13.1 Why countries/territories in the Caribbean need to co-operate

possible that would be too difficult or too expensive for a single country to carry out. Some of the institutions that have been set up to assist member countries' economies include:

1. *The Caribbean Development Bank.* The Bank lends money to farmers and manufacturers at low rates of interest to help them buy fertilizers and seeds and to set up factories. The CDB also lends money to the governments of the region to build roads, seaports and irrigation schemes.
2. *The Caribbean Investment Corporation.* This joins with member states of CARICOM (see below) and certain private citizens to set up and operate factories and farms.
3. *The Commonwealth Caribbean Technical Assistance Programme.* Under this programme the more developed Commonwealth countries send technical experts to less developed countries on request.
4. *The Caribbean Food Corporation.* This institution undertakes the production of food which is badly needed by the community. It may act alone or in co-operation with governments or private enterprise.
5. *The Caribbean Regional Youth Development Centre.* The Centre, which operates from Guyana, aims to 'promote the well-being and development of young people, who comprise the majority of the population in most countries, but whose energies are not fully harnessed, for the benefit of their societies'.

The Caribbean Community

The Caribbean Community, usually known as CARICOM, consists of Antigua, Bahamas, Barbados, Belize, Dominica, Grenada, Guyana, Haiti, Jamaica, Montserrat, St Kitts-Nevis, St Lucia, St Vincent, Surinam and Trinidad and Tobago. The British Virgin Islands and Turks and Caicos Islands participate as associate states. The Community was established by the Treaty of Chaguaramas, which set out the following arrangements:

1. A supreme body or organ, consisting of the Heads of Government of the member states, commonly called the *Conference.*
2. A *Council* of ministers responsible for the economic aspects of the Community, i.e. for the common market.
3. A body of administrative and technical officers responsible for carrying out the recommendations and decisions of the Conference and Council of ministers, known as the *Secretariat.*

The Conference finally decides on the policy of the Community and has the final word in the conclusion of treaties between the Community and international bodies and states. The Conference also settles disputes concerning the operation of the treaty, except in matters relating to the common market.

In this context 'common market' means a group arrangement in which there are no import duties on trade between one member state and another; in which one member state can export to another goods in any quantity; and in which the member states agree to place the same amount of duty on imports from countries outside the group. The Common Market Council is responsible for ensuring that the common market works effectively and for settling problems that may arise in the course of its operation. Each member state appoints one representative to the Council.

The Secretariat operates from its head office in Guyana. It is headed by the Secretary-General, who is the chief administrative officer. He is assisted by a staff of men and women drawn from the member states. The staff must accept directions from CARICOM and not from individual member countries, as they are the servants of CARICOM and not of the member states.

The Organization of Eastern Caribbean States (OECS)[1]

This organization consists of the less developed countries in CARICOM. They are Grenada, St Lucia, Dominica, Antigua, Montserrat, St Vincent and St Kitts-Nevis. The British Virgin Islands and Anguilla have associate membership. The OECS was formed on 4 July 1981, with its headquarters in Castries. It was formed primarily because the countries involved felt that they were not getting enough benefits from CARICOM.

The primary aims and objectives of the organization are:

1. To promote economic integration through the provisions of the agreement establishing the East Caribbean Common Market.
2. To promote unity and solidarity among member states and to defend their sovereignty, territorial integrity and independence.
3. To assist member states in the realization of their obligations and responsibilities to the international community.
4. To seek to achieve the fullest harmonization of foreign policy including common positions on international issues.

---

1 Condensed from an article by Jeff Hackett, 'The OECS: what it's all about', published in the *Trinidad Guardian*, 1984.

The countries of the OECS have a total population of just under 600,000. Their economies are based on tourism and agriculture. Their most notable achievement to date is the establishment of their own Central Bank.

International trade agreements

The agreement which used to be of greatest importance to Caribbean countries was *Imperial* or *Commonwealth preference*. Under this arrangement the UK agreed to buy its raw materials (most of which had to be imported) from Commonwealth countries or to charge lower import duties on such goods than on goods from other countries. In return, these countries bought most of their manufactured goods from Britain. This system lost most of its importance after Britain joined the European Economic Community (see below), but it provided an important market for West Indian sugar and bananas. France operated similar arrangements with her former colonies in the area.

1. *General Agreement on Tariffs and Trade* (GATT). There are over 70 countries in this organization. Its aim is to increase world trade by gradually reducing tariffs, and abolishing import licences and quotas.
2. *European Union* (EU). Also known as the European Common Market, this was set up by the Treaty of Rome in 1957 as the European Economic Community (EEC) and came into operation in 1958. The original members were France, (West) Germany, Italy, the Netherlands, Belgium and Luxembourg. In 1973 the UK, Republic of Ireland and Denmark joined, Greece, Spain and Portugal in 1986, and Austria, Finland and Sweden in 1995; further expansion is likely. Its aim was not only to establish a common market, as described above, but to harmonize the economic and social policies of the member states. Progress to this end has been slow, though most of the countries intend to be using a single European currency in 2002; but the Community has proved to be a very powerful economic force. Several European states have signed trade agreements with the Community and achieved Associate status.

   In response to criticisms that the Community was not doing enough to share its wealth with the underdeveloped countries, a group of *ACP* (American, Caribbean and Pacific) states was formed by the Lomé Convention. ACP states have gained limited rights of access for their agricultural products into EU markets. These rights are reviewed from time to time at joint EU/ACP conferences.
3. *European Free Trade Area* (EFTA). This was set up in 1960 between Austria, Denmark, Norway, Portugal, Sweden, Switzerland and the

UK. Iceland and Finland later joined. On joining the EEC/EU, Denmark and the UK, Portugal, and Austria, Finland and Sweden left EFTA, which now consists of Iceland, Liechtenstein, Norway and Switzerland. EFTA is purely a free-trade area; unlike a common market, it has no common external tariff.

International economic institutions

It was clear after the World War II that new means of settling international indebtedness would have to be found. Under the auspices of the United Nations, two new institutions were set up at a conference held at Bretton Woods, USA in 1944.

1. *International Monetary Fund* (IMF). The Fund is composed of gold and the currencies of the member countries; members can obtain from the Fund, in exchange for their own currencies, restricted amounts of such foreign currencies as they need to meet imbalances on their balance of payments. Each member pays a quota to the Fund; this is frequently increased as the calls on the Fund's services increase. The headquarters of the IMF are in Washington DC, USA and it is controlled by a Board of Governors on which all members are represented. Its chief aims are:
   (a) To maintain stability in the world's major trading currencies.
   (b) To reduce imbalances in international trade.
   (c) To restore confidence in the national currency of member states when it comes under pressure from speculation or economic difficulties.
2. *International Bank for Reconstruction and Development* (IBRD), also known as the *World Bank*. Its aim is to assist and encourage long-term international investment through established channels, by guaranteeing (underwriting) private investment abroad; by direct lending; and by participation in investment with commercial banks. Its most valuable function is to make loans which it thinks are good commercial risks, but where other finance is not forthcoming.

Another institution which has achieved importance in recent years is the *Organization of Petroleum Exporting Countries* (OPEC). After the Arab–Israeli War of 1973, OPEC was able to secure the agreement of its members to substantial rises in the price of oil, coupled with restrictions on output to maintain its scarcity value. The aim was to increase the revenue of oil-producing states and encourage economy in the use of a natural asset which would soon be exhausted if usage had continued to increase at pre-1973 rates. It has, however, also led to substantial price inflation and economic difficulties for many developing countries without any oil industry.

Major economic problems of the Caribbean

In spite of what has been said about economic growth and development in the islands of the Caribbean, there are quite a lot of problems that still exist. These will never be solved entirely, because hand in hand with economic growth, fresh problems will arise. For example, economic prosperity brings more cars on the roads, which were not built to take this amount of traffic. It takes time to build new roads and modernize existing ones. Meanwhile the number of cars on the roads will have grown still further and other traffic problems will occur.

Some of the main economic problems of the Caribbean are:

1. Political instability, particularly in some of the smaller islands. This holds back investment and economic growth.
2. A lack of domestic enterprise and foreign investment in some countries.
3. High unemployment, caused by lack of jobs and people not being trained to do the jobs which are in demand, e.g. too many lawyers and not enough motor mechanics.
4. Sharp rises in the prices of imported foodstuffs and other essential commodities, particularly oil.
5. Fluctuations in the business cycle, making long-term investment difficult.
6. Rapid growth of the population.
7. Strikes and industrial unrest.
8. Attempts to produce local goods to replace imports may lead to higher costs and a fall in the standard of living.
9. Natural disasters – particularly hurricanes. The eruption of the Soufriere volcano on St Vincent crippled the island's major industry, banana growing.
10. Housing shortage, as people who cannot find work in the country migrate to the towns.
11. Drug addiction and gangsterism, which harm industry and commerce.
12. Corruption in all sectors of society.

These problems present a challenge to politicians and economists. They will not be easy to solve. However, there are still good prospects for economic growth, but we will have to use all the resources available to us and all our skills. We have to develop our industries; we have to educate and train our workers; we have to change the emphasis in education to the practical and the technical; and we have to go back to the land and grow more food.

The role of education in economic development

Every territory in the Caribbean is experiencing economic evolution and in this education will play an important part. All schools – primary, secondary, vocational and technical – as well as the teacher training colleges and the Universities of the West Indies and Guyana, will have to adjust their programmes so as to meet the economic needs of the Caribbean.

The CARICOM governments have all recognized the need for this change and have laid special emphasis on the following:

1. Plans to improve the supply of trained manpower.
2. Boards to improve the quality and quantity of training within industry.
3. Grants and scholarships for further education at technical colleges and universities; where the course of study needed is not available locally, grants and scholarships are awarded for courses at overseas universities.
4. Education extension programmes for adults – particularly those who have difficulty with reading and writing – are being set up.
5. Trade unions are educating their members in industrial relations.
6. Greater emphasis on technical and medical education.
7. Schools of insurance and banking are being set up to meet the needs of these two specialized fields.
8. More teachers are being trained.
9. Interchanges of ideas and personnel with other countries. For instance, teachers from the Caribbean go to the UK and vice versa.
10. More opportunities are being given to women in education and at work.
11. Better schools with up-to-date facilities (particularly laboratories and workshops) are being provided.
12. New examinations at all levels (such as those of the Caribbean Examinations Council) are being set up to meet the local needs.
13. More textbooks and other educational aids are being provided, many specially designed for the Caribbean.
14. Regional co-operation in education, to avoid wasteful duplication of effort and improve mobility and labour.
15. Regular surveys of educational facilities and requirements.

Some of these are being provided at the national level, others are international.

Local and foreign investment

The importance of investment has been stressed several times. Without it there would be no economic advance. Investment can take many forms: public (governmental) or private; small-scale or large-scale; short-term or long-term; local or foreign. Some investments are also much safer than others; for instance, if you buy government bonds or put your money on fixed deposit with a reputable bank, there is little or no risk. If you invest in stocks and shares of private companies, there is some risk that you may lose your money entirely, or have your investment decline in value, and dividends may not be paid. Perhaps the greatest risk of all is investing in your own business.

Many industrial processes are very expensive and complicated, involving massive investment. Caribbean governments – particularly of the smaller countries – have no alternative but to go outside their borders for finance. The foreign investment may take the form of a loan from the World Bank or a similar institution, or a direct investment by a foreign-owned company setting up a factory or a processing plant, perhaps with some local involvement. This has the advantage of bringing employment and wealth to the country. However, there are also disadvantages: interest has to be paid on loans, and they have eventually to be repaid, while foreign companies will expect to remit a large part of their profits abroad as a reward for their capital – all these things can put pressure on a country's balance of payments.

Many experts believe that local investment would be encouraged if there were some stock exchanges in the Caribbean dealing in companies' stocks and shares; those that exist are stock exchanges only in name. People are naturally reluctant to buy shares if there is no ready market for them when they want to sell.

There are numbers of areas for investment in, for example, Trinidad and Tobago, some of which are:

1. Commercial banks.
2. Trust companies.
3. Finance companies.
4. Stock Exchange.
5. Unit trusts.
6. Insurance companies.
7. Building and loan societies.
8. Credit unions/co-operatives.

9. Governmental banks.
10. Treasury Bills.
11. Mortgage banks.
12. Merchant banks.
13. Sou-Sou.

ACTIVITIES

Sometimes job vacancies cannot be filled because there is no one available with the right skills or qualifications. This is called a skills shortage.

Find out what skills shortages there are in your area. (Go to the local Employment or Labour Exchange and ask what skill shortages there are). Then find out what training in these skills is available in your country.

Do a role play of a job interview.

SELF-REVISION QUESTIONS

1. List the main organizations that have been set up within the Caribbean to encourage international economic co-operation.
2. What is the importance of the Treaty of Chaguaramas?
3. List the main organs of CARICOM and the functions of each.
4. What is a common market? How does it differ from a free trade area?
5. What do the initials GATT stand for? What is the function of this organization?
6. What is the relation between the ACP states and the European Union?
7. Find out the benefits (if any) that your country has received from the ACP arrangements.
8. Compare and contrast the functions of the International Monetary Fund and the World Bank.
9. What is the correct name of the World Bank?
10. Find one country that has received assistance from the IMF. What form did this take?
11. What is OPEC? Find the names of six member states.
12. List the major economic problems facing the Caribbean. Which do you think are the most important from your own country's point of view?

13. Why is education important in economic development? Give examples of how it can help.
14. What is meant by adult illiteracy? Find out what is being done in your country to eliminate this.
15. Imagine that a new textile mill is to be built. State, with reasons, which type of investment you think would be best:
    (a) From the government.
    (b) From local private industry.
    (c) A loan from a foreign bank.
    (d) Ownership by a large foreign textile company.

APPENDIX 1

Multiple-choice questions

Choose the alternative which you think is correct. To each question there is only one correct answer.

1. The profits from a co-operative society are shared:
   (a) among the shareholders in proportion to their shareholding.
   (b) among the shareholders in proportion to their purchases.
   (c) among the customers in proportion to their purchases.
   (d) among the employees in proportion to their wages.
2. A bonded warehouse is used to store goods:
   (a) which are liable to be stolen.
   (b) which are controlled by the government.
   (c) which are subsidized by the government.
   (d) which are liable to duty and on which duty has not yet been paid.
3. Limited liability means that the shareholders:
   (a) are responsible for all the debts of the company up to their private possessions.
   (b) are responsible for all the debts of the company up to the amount that they have already contributed.
   (c) are not responsible for any debts of the company except those sanctioned at an annual general meeting.
   (d) are responsible for all the debts of the company up to the nominal value of their shareholdings.
4. The tax levied on many imported goods is called:
   (a) purchase tax.
   (b) customs duty.
   (c) excise duty.
   (d) corporation tax.
5. The maximum number of partners is:
   (a) 2
   (b) 10
   (c) 20
   (d) 50
6. The maximum number of members of a private company is:
   (a) 2
   (b) 10
   (c) 20
   (d) 50

7. Turnover means:
   (a) total credit sales.
   (b) total cash sales.
   (c) total cash and credit sales
   (d) total purchases and sales.
8. Overdrafts are given to holders of:
   (a) savings accounts.
   (b) current accounts.
   (c) deposit accounts.
   (d) fixed deposit accounts.
9. Bills of lading are used for transport by:
   (a) cargo liners only.
   (b) cargo and passenger liners.
   (c) all ships.
   (d) specially built ships only.
10. If Mr B is overcharged $60 by Mr A, Mr A will send to Mr B:
   (a) a blll of exchange.
   (b) a debit note.
   (c) a promissory note.
   (d) a credit note.
11. If goods are purchased for $120 and sold for $150, the mark-up is:
   (a) 10%
   (b) 25%
   (c) 15 %
   (d) 33⅓%
12. In Question 11, the percentage gross profit on selling price is:
   (a) 10%
   (b) 25%
   (c) 20 %
   (d) 33⅓%
13. Cash discount is allowed when payment is made:
   (a) in cash.
   (b) in advance.
   (c) at the time the goods are handed over.
   (d) within a specific period.
14. Which of the following documents is not required to register a private company?
   (a) memorandum of association.
   (b) articles of association.
   (c) prospectus.
   (d) statement of authorized capital.
15. A certificate of incorporation authorizes a public company to:
   (a) begin business.
   (b) allot shares to the public.
   (c) issue its prospectus.
   (d) issue share certificates.
16. Cheques can be drawn on:
   (a) fixed deposit account.
   (b) savings account.

(c) current account.
(d) Post Office Savings Bank account.

17. In a large department store, one would apply for a job to the:
(a) managing director.
(b) despatch department.
(c) personnel department.
(d) wages department.

18. The minimum number of members of a public company is:
(a) 7
(b) 10
(c) 2
(d) 5

19. A retailer buys an article for $130 and marks it up 30%. The selling price is:
(a) $160
(b) $159
(c) $169
(d) $180

20. A monopoly exists when there is:
(a) one buyer.
(b) one seller.
(c) one buyer and two sellers.
(d) one seller and no buyer.

21. Which of the following would you consider to be an entrepreneur?
(a) the manager of a coconut estate.
(b) a bank manager.
(c) the proprietor of a shop.
(d) a buyer in a department store.

22. Which of the following risks can a business manager not insure against?
(a) bad management.
(b) bad debts.
(c) burglary.
(d) loss of profits caused by fire.

23. Which of the following is compulsory?
(a) life assurance.
(b) fire insurance.
(c) motor vehicle insurance.
(d) fidelity guarantee insurance.

24. Which of the following is an indirect tax?
(a) petrol duty.
(b) estate duty.
(c) income tax.
(d) capital gains tax.

25. Which of the following statements is true?
(a) Trade means the buying and selling of goods.
(b) Trade means the buying and selling of goods and services.
(c) Trade means the selling of goods.
(d) Trade means the selling of goods and services.

26. Which of the following can have its shares traded on a stock exchange?
(a) a co-operative society.

(b) a public company.
(c) a private company.
(d) a partnership.

27. Trading on a stock exchange is undertaken by a:
(a) jobber.
(b) factor.
(c) underwriter.
(d) del credere agent.

28. A shop steward is an official of a:
(a) trade union.
(b) credit union.
(c) department store.
(d) political party.

29. A proforma invoice is:
(a) used to show a possible buyer exactly what he has to pay.
(b) sent out as a reminder when payment of the original invoice is overdue.
(c) sent out as a receipt when the original invoice is returned.
(d) retained in the office for book-keeping purposes.

30. A free port is:
(a) the name of the main port in the Bahamas.
(b) a port where no charge is made for the use of the facilities.
(c) a port where all ships are allowed to enter freely.
(d) a port where no duty is charged on imports.

31. Statutory companies are formed by:
(a) an Act of Parliament.
(b) Royal Charter.
(c) registration by the Registrar of Companies.
(d) voluntary agreement among the shareholders.

32. In which occupational group would you place a sugar cane cutter?
(a) direct services.
(b) extractive industry.
(c) commerce.
(d) non-productive services.

33. Division of labour means that:
(a) the same job is done by several different persons.
(b) the same job is done in several different factories.
(c) one job is split up into several different processes.
(d) labour is divided among the factors of production.

34. Professional people go into partnership because:
(a) they cannot form themselves into companies.
(b) they need their partners' advice and experience.
(c) they prefer that type of business.
(d) they are not allowed to do business alone.

35. National Insurance contributions are paid by:
(a) the employee alone.
(b) the employer alone.
(c) all taxpayers.
(d) both the employer and the employee.

36. A department store is best described as:
    (a) a store having several branches.
    (b) a store having several departments.
    (c) a store selling a variety of goods.
    (d) a store selling large items.
37. A man works for $2.50 an hour. In addition to his regular working week of 40 hours, he works overtime, 4 hours at time-and-half and 3 hours at double time. His total wages for the week are:
    (a) $160
    (b) $150
    (c) $140
    (d) $130
38. Preference shares are so called because the owners are allowed preference over others:
    (a) in purchasing more shares.
    (b) in disposing of their shares.
    (c) in allocation of dividends.
    (d) in becoming directors.
39. From which of the following institutions can one buy a money order?
    (a) commercial bank.
    (b) post office.
    (c) revenue office.
    (d) finance company.
40. Production is considered complete when the finished article is in the hands of:
    (a) the manufacturer.
    (b) the wholesaler.
    (c) the retailer.
    (d) the consumer.
41. The function of breaking bulk is performed by the:
    (a) wholesaler.
    (b) retailer.
    (c) manufacturer.
    (d) co-operative society.
42. A variety chain store is best described as:
    (a) a store having the characteristics of both multiple and department stores.
    (b) a store selling a wide range of inexpensive goods.
    (c) a store giving restricted services.
    (d) a store in which the selling staff take payments and wrap up purchases.
43. The person in whose name a cheque is made out is the:
    (a) drawer.
    (b) drawee.
    (c) payer.
    (d) payee.
44. Brokerage is:
    (a) compensation paid by insurance companies for broken glass.
    (b) commission due to a broker.
    (c) rent received from a broker.
    (d) compensation for breach of contract.

45. Production may be defined as:
    (a) creation of utility.
    (b) transforming goods into better form.
    (c) the art of satisfying human needs.
    (d) making manufactured goods.
46. Which of the following is an example of primary production?
    (a) agriculture.
    (b) textiles manufacture.
    (c) road construction.
    (d) space exploration.
47. Capital, as a factor of production, includes:
    (a) expertise of a craftsman.
    (b) raw materials.
    (c) machinery.
    (d) wealth.
48. A retailer may be defined as a trader who:
    (a) sells goods in small quantities.
    (b) buys goods from a wholesaler.
    (c) sells goods to the consumer.
    (d) buys goods in large quantities.
49. Multiple shops are:
    (a) a number of shops under one roof.
    (b) a number of shops selling similar things scattered in different parts of the city run by one company.
    (c) a number of shops selling different items but run by one company.
    (d) shops that cater for everything that a customer may ask for.
50. A wholesaler may be defined as a trader who:
    (a) sells goods to another trader.
    (b) buys goods in very large quantities.
    (c) buys goods from the producer.
    (d) sells goods to customers.
51. Which of the following dealings is not a commercial transaction?
    (a) a wholesaler buys goods for cash.
    (b) a wholesaler sells goods for cash.
    (c) a wholesaler pays wages to his workers.
    (d) a wholesaler dismisses one of his workers.
52. Which of the following items will usually not be shown on an invoice?
    (a) gross price of the goods sold.
    (b) trade discount allowed.
    (c) amount due on a previous sale.
    (d) the name of the buyer.
53. A buys 100 packets of a certain brand of cigarettes from B. Gross price per packet is $3. Trade discount is 20%. What amount of money will be shown in the invoice as net amount due?
    (a) $240
    (b) $300
    (c) $80
    (d) $2.40

54. A list of items stocked by a trader showing prices for each is called a:
   (a) invoice.
   (b) quotation.
   (c) price list.
   (d) tender.

55. I bought 50 units of a certain commodity from the manufacturer. The gross price is $10 per item and trade discount is allowed at 20%. If I settle the debt within 30 days I will be allowed a cash discount of 2%. I intend to pay immediately. How much should I pay?
   (a) $500
   (b) $390
   (c) $400
   (d) $392

56. A document listing the contents of a box being delivered is called a:
   (a) delivery note.
   (b) credit note.
   (c) package sheet.
   (d) invoice.

57. A credit note is issued to correct:
   (a) any error in an invoice.
   (b) an overcharge in an invoice.
   (c) an undercharge in an invoice.
   (d) an overcharge in a statement.

58. Earnings made by British banks in Barbados are .... Barbados
   (a) a visible import for ...
   (b) an invisible import for ...
   (c) a visible export from ...
   (d) an invisible export from ...

59. If Jamaica exports more goods to Guyana than it imports from the same country, its:
   (a) overall balance of trade will be favourable.
   (b) balance of trade with Guyana is favourable.
   (c) balance of payments is bound to be favourable.
   (d) balance of payments with Guyana is bound to be favourable.

60. Which of the following statements is true?
   (a) Balance of trade is the same as balance of payments.
   (b) Balance of payments is the difference between the imports and exports of goods by a country.
   (c) A favourable balance of trade necessarily means a favourable balance of payments.
   (d) Balance of trade is the excess of visible imports over visible exports or vice versa.

61. A bill of lading has three functions. Which of the following is not a function of a bill of lading?
   (a) It acts as an agreement between the importer and the exporter.
   (b) It serves as an agreement between the shipper and the consignor/consignee.
   (c) It serves as a proof that the goods are on board.
   (d) It acts as a title to goods.

62. Which of the following warehouses is a bonded warehouse?
    (a) a warehouse owned by a wholesaler.
    (b) a warehouse owned by a businessman which he has leased to the government.
    (c) a warehouse owned and managed by a government.
    (d) a warehouse where imported goods are held till duty is paid on them
63. Which of the following documents is used to deposit money in a current account:
    (a) a cheque.
    (b) a paying-in slip.
    (c) a credit note.
    (d) a pass book.
64. Three of the following statements apply to savings accounts. Which one does not?
    (a) Interest is allowed on deposits.
    (b) A minimum balance must be maintained at all times.
    (c) Deposits can be made only once a week.
    (d) A pass book is provided.
65. If a cheque bears an ordinary crossing it must:
    (a) be deposited in the account of the payee.
    (b) be cashed across the bank counter.
    (c) be deposited in a bank account.
    (d) be signed by the drawer on the back.
66. Endorsing a cheque means:
    (a) signing a cheque on its face.
    (b) presenting it for payment.
    (c) signing a cheque on its back.
    (d) cancelling a cheque.
67. If a person wishes to pay a number of people with one cheque he may ask his bank to do so. This service is called:
    (a) standing order.
    (b) credit transfer.
    (c) travellers' cheques.
    (d) overdraft.
68. Three of the following functions are performed by the central banks in the Caribbean. Which one is not?
    (a) They are sole currency issuing authorities.
    (b) They advise governments on financial matters.
    (c) They act as bankers to commercial banks.
    (d) They provide banking facilities to citizens.
69. Fiduciary issue means that the Central Bank has issued currency notes:
    (a) without any authority from the government.
    (b) without holding any reserves against the issue.
    (c) in more quantity than are required in the country.
    (d) in place of old notes.
70. Three of the following statements are true of a bill of exchange. Which one is not?
    (a) It must be signed by the drawee.
    (b) It must bear appropriate stamp duty.

(c) It must be signed by the drawer.
(d) It must be payable on demand.

71. Which of the following methods of payment is not made available by a commercial bank?
(a) cheque.
(b) bank draft.
(c) credit transfer.
(d) money order.

72. In event of a total loss, insurance companies undertake to pay:
(a) the sum insured.
(b) the real value of the property destroyed.
(c) the sum insured or the real value, whichever is less.
(d) the sum insured or the real value, whichever is more.

73. Which of the following documents is the principal document in an insurance contract?
(a) policy.
(b) cover note.
(c) proposal form.
(d) receipt.

74. Which means of transport will you recommend for transporting flowers from Kingston to London?
(a) air.
(b) sea.
(c) land.
(d) railway.

75. Which medium of advertising is most suitable to advertise a new brand of typewriters?
(a) radio.
(b) newspapers.
(c) television.
(d) direct contact with probable customers.

76. Three of the following statements are true of a sole trader. Which one is not?
(a) He invests all the capital.
(b) He bears all losses and takes all profits.
(c) He must manage his business alone.
(d) His liability is unlimited.

77. A limited partner:
(a) takes an active part in the management of the firm.
(b) is not entitled to any profits.
(c) does not bear any losses.
(d) bears losses only to a stated sum.

78. In the absence of a partnership agreement partners should:
(a) share profits and losses in the ratio of their capitals.
(b) not be allowed any interest or any loans advanced to them by the business.
(c) not be allowed to inspect the books of account.
(d) not be paid any interest on capital contributed by them.

79. I hold one share in a public limited company which is limited by shares. The nominal value of the share is $20. The company has called $14 on the share but I have paid only $11 on it. If the company goes into liquidation today the maximum amount of money I may be asked to contribute is:
   (a) $20
   (b) $3
   (c) $6
   (d) $9
80. A public limited company was formed and registered with a share capital of $200,000 divided into 10,000 ordinary shares of equal value. A month after registration the company asked for applications to issue shares. They asked for $4 per share as application money, $3 per share as allotment money and $5 per share as first call. By the end of the third month they had issued 6,000 shares against which application moncy, allotment money and first call has been paid except for 100 shares on which first call was outstanding. What will be the issues capital of the company on that date?
   (a) $120,000
   (b) $72,000
   (c) $71,500
   (d) $200,000
81. Facts as above. What will be the paid-up capital of the company on that date?
   (a) $120,000
   (b) $72,000
   (c) $71,500
   (d) $200,000
82. Facts as above. Calculate the called-up capital of the company as at that date.
   (a) $120,000
   (b) $72,000
   (c) $71,500
   (d) $200,000
83. An unfavourable balance of trade is when:
   (a) imports exceed exports.
   (b) exports exceed imports.
   (c) exports and imports are equal.
   (d) imports increase in price relative to exports.
84. The manufacture of large quantities of similar goods is called:
   (a) the division of labour.
   (b) consumption.
   (c) mass production.
   (d) the chain of production.
85. The abbreviated phase 'E & O E' is likely to be found at the bottom of:
   (a) a receipt.
   (b) an invoice.
   (c) a cheque.
   (d) a delivery note.
86. Which of the following provides a direct service to the consumer?
   (a) manufacturer.

(b) lumberjack.
(c) solicitor.
(d) dock worker.

87. Insurance against loss of money stolen by an employee in a position of trust is called:
(a) marine insurance.
(b) employer's liability insurance.
(c) fidelity guarantee insurance.
(d) National Insurance.

88. A form of retailing frequently described as a collection of shops under one roof is:
(a) mail order house.
(b) department store.
(c) multiple store.
(d) supermarket.

89. A loss leader is:
(a) a free gift with a purchase.
(b) a claims manager of an insurance company.
(c) an article sold cheaply to attract customers into the store.
(d) an editorial column in *The Daily Gleaner.*

90. If you want your bank to pay a fixed amount for you every month to the same person, the most convenient method is to:
(a) ask the bank to lend you the money.
(b) send the bank a cheque.
(c) arrange a bank overdraft.
(d) give the bank a standing order.

91. The bank on which a cheque is drawn is called the:
(a) drawee.
(b) drawer.
(c) payee.
(d) payer.

92. The exchange of goods without money is called:
(a) credit sale.
(b) hire purchase.
(c) barter.
(d) deferred payment.

93. In which class of occupation would you place a dentist?
(a) extractive industry.
(b) manufacturing industry.
(c) commerce.
(d) direct services.

94. Liners carry cargo:
(a) on fixed routes.
(b) at regular times.
(c) to and from any port.
(d) for export only.

95. Information requested from a bank concerning the credit-worthiness of a new customer to a business is known as a:
(a) letter of credit.

(b) general enquiry.
(c) status enquiry.
(d) directory enquiry.

96. Which is the quickest way of sending money to someone in another town? Is it:
(a) registered post.
(b) postal order.
(c) telegraphic money order.
(d) cheque.

97. The allowance given to customers to encourage them to pay promptly is called:
(a) cash discount.
(b) trade discount.
(c) dividend.
(d) commission.

98. If goods are bought on HP they become the property of the purchaser after:
(a) the first payment.
(b) taking possession.
(c) signing the contract.
(d) the last payment.

99. The purpose of an invoice is to:
(a) acknowledge receipt of goods.
(b) inform the buyer of the cost of the goods supplied.
(c) tell the buyer what goods are available.
(d) order goods from the supplier.

Answers to multiple-choice questions

	1. b	2. d	3. d	4. b	5. c	6. d	7. c	8. b	9. c
10. d	11. b	12. c	13. d	14. c	15. c	16. c	17. c	18. a	19. c
20. b	21. c	22. a	23. c	24. a	25. b	26. b	27. a	28. a	29. a
30. d	31. a	32. b	33. c	34. a	35. d	36. b	37. d	38. c	39. b
40. d	41. a	42. a	43. d	44. b	45. a	46. a	47. c	48. c	49. b
50. a	51. d	52. c	53. a	54. c	55. d	56. c	57. b	58. b	59. b
60. d	61. a	62. d	63. b	64. c	65. c	66. c	67. b	68. d	69. b
70. d	71. d	72. c	73. a	74. a	75. d	76. c	77. d	78. d	79. d
80. a	81. c	82. b	83. a	84. c	85. b	86. c	87. c	88. b	89. c
90. d	91. a	92. c	93. d	94. c	95. c	96. c	97. a	98. d	99. b

APPENDIX 2

Specimen test papers

A. Basic

1½ hours allowed

Answer any FOUR questions.

1. (a) List the SIX essential features of a valid contract.
   (b) What is a specialty contract? Give THREE examples.
2. (a) What are the advantages to the consumer of buying goods on hire purchase? Are there any disadvantages?
   (b) Vijay can buy a motorbike on H.P. for $200 deposit and 12 monthly payments of $100. The cash price is $1,000 but he would have to borrow the money from a bank at 20% interest for one year. Which alternative is best? Give your reasons.
3. (a) What is the difference between a central bank and a clearing bank?
   (b) List SIX functions performed by a central bank.
4. List FOUR types of tax levied in your country and give FOUR examples of the way in which the government spends the money raised by taxation.
5. What are the principal factors affecting the location of industry in the Caribbean?
6. What is meant by elasticity of demand? Give two examples each of goods demand for which is (a) elastic and (b) inelastic.
7. (a) What is an 'underdeveloped country'?
   (b) List the main factors that hold back economic development.

B. General

2¼ hours allowed

Section I – Answer all SIX questions.

1. Fred has been trading as a shopkeeper for many years. He wishes to expand the business and his sister-in-law has agreed to provide extra capital.
   (a) He is undecided whether to form a partnership or a limited company. Advise him on the advantages and disadvantages of each form of organization.
   (b) If he decides to form a limited company, list the steps he must take.
2. Mr Bynoe falls sick after eating a nationally advertised brand of meat pie which his wife has bought from a local supermarket. As a result, he is off work for tvo weeks. Advise him of the various forms of legal action which could be taken.
3. The Universal Trading Co. receives a large order from a customer in another island. Hitherto business with this customer has been on a small scale only.
   (a) Explain the principal terms of supply in an export transaction.

(b) What precautions should a trader take before supplying goods on credit?
(c) State the shipping procedures and documents required if UTC decides to supply the goods on a 'documentary credit' basis.

4. Excelsior Manufacturing Ltd produce plastic dustbins, housewares and office sundries by a hot moulding process in small galvanized iron sheds which were formerly part of an army barracks. Despite paying good wages, management is worried by absenteeism, high labour turnover and declining output.
Discuss the factors which may have led to this situation and suggest steps that might be taken to effect improvements.

5. Draw up an organization chart for the Seaview Hotel based on the following information.
Under the board of directors, the hotel is divided into six departments (Reception and Finance; Kitchen; Food Service; Housekeeping; Laundry; and Maintenance) and run by a General Manager and an Assistant General Manager.
In charge of the Reception and Finance Department is a Financial Controller, assisted by receptionists, porters, accountants and two food and beverage controllers.
The kitchens are in charge of the Chef de Cuisine, assisted by four Chefs de Partie and one Relief Chef.
The Food Service Department is run by the Maître d'Hôtel, controlling restaurant waiters, floor service waiters and barmen.
The Housekeeper controls chambermaids and cleaners, while the Laundry is divided into two sections, Linen and General.
The Maintenance Department is run by the Chief Engineer, controlling an electrician, a plumber, security guards and gardeners.

6. Stephen Lee is a self-employed electrician. He is concerned about:
(a) Providing an income for his wife and children should he die.
(b) Replacing tools or equipment that are lost or stolen.
(c) Providing for his retirement.
In each case, explain the insurance services which could help Mr Lee.

Section II – Answer any TWO questions.

7. 'The obligations of a business to its customers, its employees and the government are now more important than its obligation to shareholders.' Discuss.

8. List the main international organizations that affect governments in the Caribbean and write brief notes on the functions of each.

9. (a) What are the main advertising media available to manufacturers of consumer products in the Caribbean?
(b) It is often stated that the costs of advertising are passed on to consumers in the form of higher prices. Do you agree? Give reasons.

10. (a) How is a country's balance of payments calculated? How is a deficit on balance of payments financed?
(b) List THREE measurements a government may take to correct an unsatisfactory balance-of-payments position, giving the advantages and disadvantages of each.

Index